Breathes there a car collector or enthusiast out there who doesn't possess at least one miniature version of a favorite automobile? We take a look, this issue, at the charming world of the ⅟₄₃ model. One of them, a Chrysler Airflow by Brooklin, appears on our cover, the photograph taken by Stan Grayson with the assistance of art director Ted Hall. Our model story includes vehicles of all eras. Additional stories this issue begin with motoring's first decade and follow through to 1980. We start with a look at a trio which gave its initials to a motorcar. The E-M-F proved rather more robust than the company building it and Messrs. Everitt, Metzger and Flanders had their share of ups and downs. Still, they achieved more success than many others. Consider Bucciali, a mystery of the classic era which has never been better unravelled than in Griff Borgeson's piece at issue's end.

Not quite as mysterious but often inscrutable are the workings of the Ferrari factory. We are fortunate to present the story of Mauro Forghieri, one of Ferrari's chief lieutenants of the past two decades. From a pre-Ferrari world comes the five-liter Bugatti gracing our contents page and photographed by Neill Bruce. We first saw the car crackling up Shelsley Walsh in July 1978 and thought you'd enjoy knowing about it. Far removed from the Bugatti was the Falcon entered in the Monte Carlo Rally in 1963 and '64. That colorful story is told here too. There's also an in-depth look at the newest Lincoln, a car designed for a changing world. Our stories, then, come from almost every automotive era. It has been given to few men to be part of them all. One who was is Sammy Davis. Recounted here is the life story of this inimitable old gentleman. During his career he drove some of history's greatest cars and was witness to many of motoring's greatest events. It's all enough to make even the most mild-mannered of enthusiasts slightly British green with envy.

aUTOMOBILE
Quarterly

The Connoisseur's Magazine of Motoring Today, Yesterday and Tomorrow

Fourth Quarter 1979   Volume XVII, Number 4

PUBLISHER AND PRESIDENT:
L. SCOTT BAILEY

EDITOR:
BEVERLY RAE KIMES

SENIOR EDITOR:
STAN GRAYSON

EUROPEAN EDITOR:
GRIFFITH BORGESON

CONTRIBUTING EDITORS:
ANGELO TITO ANSELMI, WILLIAM BODDY,
RUSS CATLIN, ALLAN GIRDLER,
KARL LUDVIGSEN, DAVID OWEN, CARL WAGNER

PHOTOGRAPHERS:
GIORGIO BELLIA, RICHARD A. BROWN,
GIORGIO BOSCHETTI, NEILL BRUCE, RICK LENZ,
CARL MALOTKA, CHARLES MILLER, ROY QUERY,
STANLEY ROSENTHALL, JULIUS WEITMANN

PRODUCTION EDITOR:
MARY B. WILLIAMS

BUSINESS MANAGER:
KEVIN G. BITZ

ART DIRECTOR:
THEODORE R.F. HALL

ASSISTANT ART DIRECTOR:
MICHAEL PARDO

CHIEF OF RESEARCH:
HENRY AUSTIN CLARK, JR.

RESEARCH ASSOCIATES:
CHARLES L. BETTS, JR., JAMES J. BRADLEY,
LESLIE R. HENRY, U.S.A.
MICHAEL SEDGWICK, GREAT BRITAIN
GIANNI ROGLIATTI, ITALY; NICHOLAS FRANCO, JR., SPAIN

ARTISTS:
THOMAS E. FORNANDER, WALTER GOTSCHKE,
PETER HELCK, YOSHIHIRO INOMOTO,
JOHN PECKHAM, KEN RUSH

CIRCULATION MANAGER:
JOHN HEFFELFINGER

VICE-PRESIDENT:
MARGARET T. BAILEY

Automobile Quarterly is published quarterly by Automobile Quarterly, Inc., in association with the Princeton Institute for Historic Research. Editorial Offices: 221 Nassau Street, Princeton, New Jersey 08540. Office of Publication: 245 West Main Street, Kutztown, Pennsylvania 19530. Telephone: 215-683-8352. Automobile Quarterly is printed in the United States by the Kutztown Publishing Company on Mead Offset Enamel paper; color separations by Lincoln Graphics Incorporated, Cherry Hill, New Jersey; binding by National Publishing Company, Philadelphia, Pennsylvania.
Single copies $10.95; annual subscription $38.00. Four-Year Indexes (Volume I-IV, Volume V-VIII, Volume IX-XII and Volume XIII-XVI) are available at $10.95 each. All subscriptions, orders, changes of address and correspondence concerning subscriptions should be sent to 245 West Main Street, Kutztown, Pennsylvania 19530.
Second class postage paid at Kutztown, Pennsylvania and at additional mailing offices.

CONTENTS

BY BEVERLY RAE KIMES

"Every Morning Fix-it." "Every Mechanic's Friend." "Eternally Missing Fire." "Every Mechanical Fault." Alas, the E-M-F, victim of orthography, its destiny sealed the day the decision was made to make its initials its name, or more precisely the arrangement of those initials. Had Mr. M or Mr. F been chosen to be first, the wags of the day wouldn't have had nearly so merry a time maligning the car, nor would it have passed into history with a reputation unfairly tarnished by bad jokes.

"Every Morning Frustration"—a phrase not favored by the punsters—was perhaps more to the point anyway. But that had nothing to do with the car, rather the continuing contretemps of the Messrs. Everitt, Metzger and Flanders in producing it. LeRoy had his problems too. His job was publicity.

This cast of characters in the tragi-comedy that is the E-M-F story—and that of the various enterprises emanating from or attendant to it—will be presented in their order of appearance.

Enter Byron F.—everybody called him "Barney"—Everitt. He was a round sort of man, short, squat, jovial, and a whiz at making or getting money. Born in Ridgetown, Ontario in 1872, he learned the wagon-building trade in Chatham, traveled to Detroit at age nineteen, worked for carriage maker Hugh Johnson, became affiliated with the body-building enterprise of the Wilson family, started his own in 1899, received body orders first from Ransom Olds, then Henry Ford; with his business prospering hired Fred J. Fisher (one of seven brothers from Norwalk, Ohio) and Walter O. Briggs (of Ypsilanti, Michigan) to help him, and launched his own car, an assembled one called the Wayne, around 1904. But it was his coachwork which made him rich; as was said then, "he has made, painted and trimmed more automobile bodies, twice over, than any other concern." His was one of the biggest names in Detroit.

Next, William E. Metzger, born 1868 in Peru, Illinois, émigré to Michigan at age ten, and a bicycle merchant until he visited London in 1895 and attended the world's first automobile show. His enthusiasm fired, he returned to Detroit, bought a batch of electric cars, sold them, then a bunch of steamers, and did same; established what was most likely America's first automobile dealership, in Detroit, as the century was about to turn; helped stage America's earliest automobile shows, in Detroit and in New York's Madison Square Garden in 1900; was one of the prime movers in the Association of Licensed Automobile Manufacturers; promoted races at Grosse Pointe, offering a $200 prize if a cash-strapped Barney Oldfield—"I'd rather be dead than broke"—could speed Ford 999 faster over the course than Alexander and his namesake Winton; affiliated himself with the Northern Motor Car Company in 1902 and that same year was one of the organizers of the venture begun to build a car called the Cadillac, 2700 of which he took orders for at the New York Automobile Show in January 1903, before anyone knew the name and no more than three of the cars had been produced. He was tall, rather aristocratic looking, and keen of eye. He was also extraordinarily persuasive. William E. Metzger could sell anything.

Penultimately comes Walter E. Flanders, born in 1871 in Rutland, invariably described then as "a poor Vermont machinist" who became an "industrial colossus." The son of a country doctor whose fees were generally paid in farm produce, he left

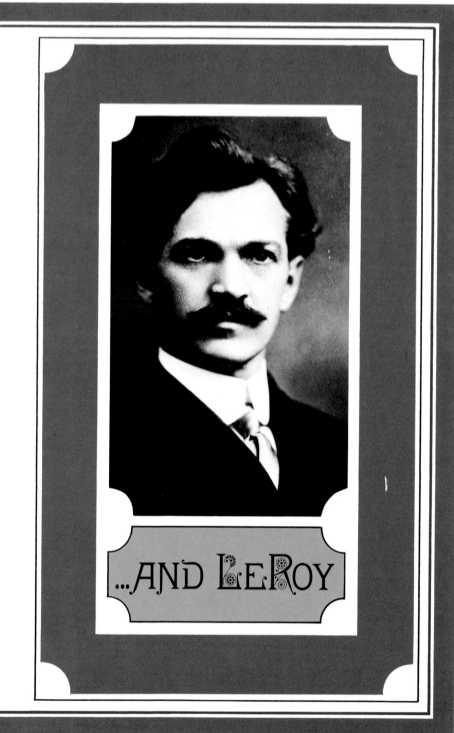

...AND LeRoy

school at fifteen to seek his fortune tending to mechanical things, for cash, including sewing machines during an apprenticeship at Singer, followed by an association with Thomas S. Walburn in general machining in Cleveland, out of which came an order from Henry Ford in Detroit for a thousand crankshafts, the order being filled and on time—a rarity in those days—this convincing Ford that Flanders was just the man to have on the team he was assembling to move his company into mass quantity manufacture of automobiles. At arranging production machinery—and inventing it as well, various multiple drill, vertical boring mill and valve grinding machines being to his credit—and in cutting supply and inventory costs, there was no one better than Walter Flanders. He wasn't interested in cars so much as building them. Those experiments with a new model in a back room at the Ford company didn't concern him; he was busy in the plant moving machines around, setting up procedures, effecting time-saving methods; he wanted to see the product only when it was ready and he didn't care if its model initial was N, R, S—or T. A huge man (close to 275 pounds) with a great shock of curly hair and a voice that, as Ford associate Charles Sorensen commented, "could be heard in a drop-forge plant," Flanders played hard and rough. A carouser and hell-raiser of epic proportion at night, he was blessed somehow with an immunity to morning-after hangovers, showing up on time at the plant every day, effectively and forthrightly directing his men, who admired him, in their work—and worrying Henry Ford a bit that the force of Flanders' personality might become a problem, that Flanders might overwhelm, and overtake, Ford in his own company.

Finally, there was LeRoy. E. LeRoy Pelletier, born in 1868 in Houlton, Maine, a man possessed of a small body, a large head, and nervous energy that was electrifying. As a newspaperman he covered the Klondike stampede for *The New York Times** and as a publicist he served as advance man for a circus—all this before settling down, initially in Buffalo, New York in 1902 to build a car called the Duquesne, and following its failure relocating in Detroit in 1905 to work for Henry Ford, first as consulting engineer and thereafter, when it became obvious he was considerably more adept with words than machines, as Ford's private secretary and advertising manager, though for the latter he apparently preferred the title "publicity engineer." That he was. A brilliant intellect matched with a vivid imagination, he could think even faster than he could talk, and his conversation was routinely described as "rapid-fire."

With the principal characters thus introduced—supporting players to follow—we move backstage. The next scene onstage is the dining room of the Cafe des Beaux Arts in New York City, but the actors in this drama must meet first to prepare their roles. We don't know exactly when all this happened, but from the facts on hand the scenario in the wings can be interpreted with assurance as the following.

"Henceforth the history of this industry will be the story of a conflict between giants," Walter Flanders was soon to say. He was thinking it already, he had decided he wanted to be one of them, and he felt this would be unlikely if he remained as production manager with the introverted but quietly and recalcitrantly dominating Ford. He was apparently unaware of Ford's fears regarding him. There was a personality clash in any case between the roistering Flanders and his puritanical em-

---

*His dispatches to the *Times*, covering the period 1897 to 1900, provide enthralling reading, Pelletier narrating tales of "precautions against starvation," "delays due to selfishness," "preventing a corner in supplies," "smallpox comes to camp," "getting ready for the greenhorns," "pistols drawn many times," "large loss of life and a murder," "no time for legal trials." They would make for a terrific adventure movie.

E·M·F *First deliveries of the Model 30 E-M-F began in September 1908; this touring car, owned by Harold Worley, was among the early ones.*

ployer. The former presented notice of his resignation to the latter, and it was accepted without regret—though Henry probably wasn't too happy that Flanders also convinced Thomas Walburn (who had traveled with him to Ford from Cleveland) and Max Wollering (a talented machinist Ford had hired upon Flanders' recommendation) to join him in the exodus from Dearborn.

Obviously, already there had been a good deal of pre-planning because the first mention of any of this in the press was a short notice in *The Motor World* edition of March 12th, 1908 announcing Flanders' new position as general manager of the Wayne Automobile Company, with the person formerly holding that title, Barney Everitt, moving up to the firm's presidency. Wayne spokesmen were quoted as proceeding with plans for the production of automobiles "on a scale heretofore unattempted." One week to the day later, Henry Ford sent a circular to his dealers announcing his new Model T.

What was happening was the same idea—mass quantity manufacture—being contemplated in two different camps, with one significant difference. Henry Ford opted for the low-priced field and a primeval automobile. Flanders who was the driving force in the rival camp believed the motoring public more likely to accept a "well finished" car and opted for the middle price range. Survival in this field, he was convinced, demanded a capital investment of a couple of million dollars. Barney Everitt could come up with half of that right away, and simply a listing of his financial angels (William T. Barbour, J.B. Gunderson, Charles L. Palm, J.B. Book), so the press

would say, "goes to show that the new company will have almost unlimited resources." It would also have the benefit of the best salesman in the business. Betimes, William E. Metzger had "retired" as sales manager of the Cadillac Motor Car Company. M was about to join E and F.

When it happened, the result was not simply announced, it was celebrated—at dinner at the Cafe des Beaux Arts on Tuesday, June 2nd, 1908. It was a gala affair, no new automobile company in the industry's history had ever been given a grander introduction, nor had any held grander promise for the future. Everitt, the financial genius. Metzger, the salesman extraordinaire. Flanders, the production man nonpareil. Interestingly, reporters often referred to them as the "Big Three." Was anything missing? Well, convincing the populace that this new company could produce a $2500 car by its mass production methods and sell the result at $1250, twice the car for half the price, required some clever writing and promotion. Flanders remembered Ford's private secretary, who had left Henry for Tarrytown, New York and Maxwell-Briscoe. LeRoy Pelletier saw the E-M-F venture as laden with gold as the Klondike and quickly joined up.

For the banquet at the Cafe des Beaux Arts, it was reported that Everitt and Metzger personally transported the frogs' legs from Detroit, Flanders saw to it that sufficient libation was at hand, and Pelletier provided the after-dinner jokes. A novel departure from standard trade banquet practice was the invitation to reporters and guests to bring along their wives and sweethearts. All in all, it was a most unusual way

an effective dealer network himself. But Barney Everitt, who took the E-M-F presidency title, was persuaded by Flanders that time was of the essence—and thus South Bend was given a role in the E-M-F act. It was a co-starring one. Studebaker would handle all of the E-M-F export business (its contacts abroad were heady) and the United States was divided in half, with Studebaker manager Hayden Eames to see to E-M-F sales in the South and the West, the rest of the country to be in the direct charge of William Metzger. And Studebaker was to take half of the E-M-F production, which was planned for 12,000 units the first year.

The pilot cars were sent down the production line in July, deliveries began in September, journalists having been given complete details regarding the E-M-F product the month previous. There was nothing extraordinary for them to report; indeed it was the ordinary nature of the E-M-F upon which LeRoy Pelletier based his advertising strategy: "Nothing added—no frills or furbelows. Nothing omitted that experience has proven or convention taught you to consider a necessary part of a first-class motorcar. Not one original feature—not a single novelty—no startling innovations. Not one experiment—not one hair-brained theory or half-baked mechanical idea—not an untried or unproven invention—or metallurgical hallucination—will you discover in the E-M-F '30'."

What was unusual about the E-M-F was its price and what the car offered for it. Its chief engineer was William E. Kelly, who had worked with Barney Everitt at Wayne. He called reporters together and said he had built his first automobile in 1895 which had "not come up to his expectations," had since been "handicapped by having to work under the 'assembled car' system," and the E-M-F was for him the realization of "a long cherished ambition." It had a four-cylinder engine (4 by 4½ bore and stroke, 226 cubic inches), the cylinders cast in pairs, with waterjackets cast integral and large mechanically operated valves. A nicety involved the valve guides which were machined and pressed into rather than cast integral with the cylinders, making replacement easy when worn. Another nicety was the splash lubrication system governed by an automatic vacuum feed (the oil reservoir cast with the aluminum crankcase), this allowing the use of large tubes and avoiding the clogged pipes so frequently resulting with gravity feed. One filling of the oil reservoir, Kelly said, was good for three to five hundred miles depending on road conditions.

The single float feed carburetor was adjustable from the driver's seat, there was a dual jump spark ignition system consisting of quadruple coil, commutator, battery and magneto built into the engine. This last was unusual for this period, the magneto frequently being considered an "accessory," but to E-M-F, "it is as much a part of the car as are the valves." Initially cooling was thermo-syphon, but after the first batch of cars was in the field, overheating problems were discovered, and William Kelly personally recalled the vehicles and installed water pumps on them, and all subsequent E-M-F's.

The car's frame was a pressed steel U-section with semi-elliptic front springs, full elliptic rear, and double-acting brakes on the rear wheels. A three-speed sliding gear transmission was incorporated into the rear axle, steering was worm and sector, and the clutch was an expanding ring. This last, incidentally, was the only significant detail which would be altered for 1910. As LeRoy Pelletier explained it matter-of-factly, "some owners simply couldn't or wouldn't master the simple knack [of the expanding ring clutch]. So it has been changed. A cone clutch, simple and also better in some respects, has been substituted . . ." That, and a wheelbase increase of two inches (to 108) and for no apparent reason, were the only refinements made after the first year's production.

to reveal the birth of a new automobile company. But then this was no ordinary new company.

Seeing to the prosaic details came next. In essence, the new Everitt-Metzger-Flanders Company represented a merger of the Wayne Automobile Company and the Northern Motor Car Company, in which William Metzger quickly and conveniently acquired a controlling interest. This provided E-M-F three ready-made plants, Wayne's and Northern's in Detroit, and the latter's second plant in Port Huron. To provide a ready-made dealership organization, E-M-F contacted the Studebaker brothers in Indiana. Since before the Civil War, the Studebakers had enjoyed preeminence in the wagon-building field, but they had ventured only cautiously into the automobile business, producing a few electrics and gasoline cars, and the coachwork for a line of pricey fours built on the Garford chassis. The E-M-F proposition seemed a marvelous opportunity for a maximum effort with minimum risk. As Colonel George M. Studebaker said at the time, "We considered it more advantageous to us to form an alliance with a group of men . . . possessing . . . factory facilities, experience and manufacturing ability of a rare order, as well as an intimate knowledge of the problems peculiar to the motorcar, than to establish a separate factory of our own." For E-M-F's part, the alliance brought 4000 dealers to the new company right away. General manager Walter Flanders was particularly pleased about that. Sales manager William Metzger was dubious, and perhaps a little chagrined that, super salesman that he was, his partners did not assume he could put together

Not that anything further was necessary. Not at all. Motoring periodicals had been uniformly astounded by the quality and value of the E-M-F. "There is nothing in the appearance of the car that would suggest scrimping or cheapness," said *Cycle and Automobile Trade Journal*. It "is fitted with every device known to the art," allowed *The Automobile. The Horseless Age* was impressed by the "extensive use of pressed steel"; no malleable castings appeared anywhere on the car. Who would have believed four cylinders, thirty horsepower, five-passenger capacity, "selective type of transmission, quick detachable tires and double ignition system for such a price," cooed *Motor Age*. "Who can doubt that the promise was kept?" asked *MoToR*.

The E-M-F promise was, as Walter Flanders said at every available opportunity, that "a better automobile can be built and sold for $1250 than is possible at twice that price." The quality was possible because of superior production facilities and methods, the price because of the quantity production. Of course, the very same day the first E-M-F's rolled out of the factory on one side of town, on the other the first Model T's rolled out of Ford, and their price tag was $400 less. But the T provided only 177 cubic inches and 20 hp, a 100-inch wheelbase, featured a planetary transmission, thermo-syphon cooling (this proved the reverse of the E-M-F experience, original T's had centrifugal water pumps but early on Henry Ford decided on the more basal thermo-syphon)—and the T could certainly not be awarded that "new descriptive term," as *The Automobile* put it, "which has come into vogue in automobiling." Everyone called the E-M-F "classy."

In 1911, when the T's price was lowered, to $780, the E-M-F's was too, to $1100. And LeRoy Pelletier who, the year before, had published a little booklet—"The Hyphen"—comprising a lengthy interview with the loquacious Flanders and containing the original slogan simply changed that quote to "a better automobile can be built and sold for $1100 than is possible at twice the price" and ran the rest of the interview again virtually verbatim. Except for the deletion of one significant sentence: "We propose being the largest builders of automobiles in the world."

The number of E-M-F cars produced to December 1909 totaled 8132—though the year following this would be raised to 15,300. (Model T production for the same period was a little more than double that.) There was the bright spot of the E-M-F providing the "path-finding" for the Glidden Tour of 1909, however—which provided LeRoy Pelletier grand promotional possibilities, all of which he took advantage. Look at the pictures, he said when the trek from Detroit to Denver that April was over, "The car looks as if the stunt was nuts to her. Nothing about her, not even the varnish on the body, indicates that she has been through anything more than a pretty strenuous tour—such as you will want to make with the car you buy. There's nothing broken, not even a fender bent. We didn't resort to any of the clever (?) little tricks practiced by some publicity promoters, of shooting holes in the body, scratching up the paint, and breaking lamps and fenders just to make her look like a tramp. Nor did we leave mud on her till it caked four inches deep. It wasn't necessary to manufacture hardships on this trip, or to fake up injuries to prove she had had adventures. These there were in plenty, as all the world knows. The steering gear never failed, so she wasn't ditched. The brakes never failed to hold, so she always stopped when necessary and didn't bump lamps or radiator. The radiator is properly suspended, so it didn't spring a leak. Frame is extra heavy, so it didn't sag. Fenders are properly made and attached, so they are still in place as on the day she started out."

And the car was washed every night so it would always look "classy" like an E-M-F should. The AAA Contest Board's official "pathfinder," Dai Lewis, said he had been skeptical about "starting on such a trip in a car that was new to the market," but af-

terwards told Pelletier that he was ashamed of his doubts: "You can quote me as saying the E-M-F '30' is a wonderful car." Pelletier did—as often as possible.

Because by now the jibes about the initials had begun—and most of them were heard first in the showrooms of the competition. Pelletier tried to write away the problem. Competitors have said some very cutting things, he noted in one leaflet, "that is, they were intended to be cutting . . . oh, they were awfully peevish. . . . We understood that and so laughed over their lame jokes more heartily than they did themselves. The intended victim can always laugh at a joke that misses the mark." Perhaps . . . but LeRoy didn't sound very convincing.

And what was happening behind the scenes was no laughing matter at all. The partners were quarreling. And it was over Studebaker. Metzger had not favored the alliance from the beginning, and now he convinced Everitt that it had been a bad idea too. Flanders, scarcely the diplomatic sort, huffed and puffed—and literally blew the partnership away. In May of 1909 it was revealed that the E and the M of E-M-F were leaving the company, selling out their interest to the Studebaker brothers who would handle all E-M-F distribution after September 1st. The cash amount tendered Everitt and Metzger has since been bandied about as in the million-dollar range, which was wildly inflated, the actual amount was less than half that ($362,500), which was still a tidy enough sum for the two to venture off and start a new company to build a new car. Which they did. Taking along engineer William Kelly to help.

One matter was seen to immediately. No initials this time, that was for certain, but Everitt-Metzger or Metzger-Everitt was an unwieldy and certainly not euphonious mouthful, so the partners decided instead that the car would be called the Everitt and it would be built by the Metzger Motor Car Company. With the billing thus solved, the new firm was incorporated for a half-million dollars on September 20th, 1909, the factory of the truck-manufacturing Jacob Meier Company in Detroit was purchased, and William Kelly was put to work designing what would be built there.

It was essentially an E-M-F, it was even called a "30," but there was one departure of note. As Len Shaw would write in the *Cycle and Automobile Trade Journal*, "The four cylinders are cast together, but in this instance the en bloc principle has been carried to an extreme that gives the powerplant a distinctiveness while the most gruelling tests have demonstrated the correctness of the theory and its application." The main casting included the cylinders, the upper half of the crankcase, intake and exhaust manifolds, the inner half of the gear housing, the upper half of the bearing beds—and for 1911 the magneto and pump supports would be added as well. In addition, the stroke was a quarter of an inch longer, the wheelbase was set at 110 inches, its price was tagged a hundred dollars more—but other than that one could read the E-M-F 30 specs and learn everything there was to know about the Everitt 30.

"The Car for You" and "A Car with a Rich and Rare Heritage," the ads ballyhooed—obviously Everitt and Metzger could have used the services of LeRoy Pelletier—and in a calculated dig at the motorcar which still bore their initials, it was noted that the "Everitt '30' motor contains 150 fewer parts than its closest competitor! Think of it—150 less parts!" Advertising also backdated William Kelly's maiden horseless carriage venture to 1891 and described it as "one of the first practical cars ever built." Pelletier would never have allowed such nonsense.

The prominence of its builders insured a ready acceptance of the car initially, and the planned output of 2500 units for 1910 was pre-sold before production even began. Thus assured, the Messrs. Everitt and Metzger proceeded to purchase the Hewitt Motor Company of New York, scuttling that firm's automobile but retaining its truck production, and sold rights to manufacture the Everitt in Canada to the Tudhope

Motor Company. But within a year the Hewitt alliance was, as *The Motor World* headlined, "unmerged," with Edward R. Hewitt henceforth building his own trucks in his own new factory at West End Avenue and 64th Street in New York. The Canadian connection proved similarly unfruitful.

For 1912 the Everitt home market looked far more promising, and all attention was focused on it. Presented now were three models: the returning 4-30, dropped in price to $1250; the newish 4-36 on a 115-inch wheelbase at $1500; and the brand-new Six-48 on a 127-inch wheelbase which was a whopping lot of car for $1850. The Everitt fours and the six all shared the 4 by 4¾ bore and stroke dimension with which the marque had been born, and each was simply a bigger or smaller clone of the other. The "All-Chrome-Nickel Steel Car" was one tagline, the "Self-Starting Everitt" was another. (Like Chalmers and Winton and others, Everitt had a fling with a compressed air device which Cadillac would soon render obsolete.) The press was uniformly laudatory, and indeed provided catchier phrases of commendation than the Metzger publicity department could come up with. "Idealized the real, and then realized the ideal" was offered by *Motor Age*. Overall, Barney Everitt and William Metzger were rather pleased with the way things appeared to be moving along.

Meanwhile, Walter Flanders was having an awful time of it at E-M-F, where now he was both president and general manager. Firstly, he was mightily nettled by Henry Ford who was under-selling him and out-producing him in a factory the production setup for which had largely been his doing. Consequently, in July 1909, he talked the Studebakers into helping him buy the DeLuxe Motor Company, whose high-priced car had been given a death rattle soon after birth, but whose Detroit plant was admirably situated and equipped. Several other companies were interested in it as well but as *The Automobile* reported, "Walter Flanders shattered all previous

E·M·F *Posed in front of the home of "Hoosier Poet" James Whitcomb Riley in Indianapolis, this 1909 Model 30 E-M-F is owned by Harold B. Casey.*

speed records by opening negotiations in the morning and turning over the cash in the afternoon [$800,000 was the widely-guessed figure, neither confirmed nor denied], closing the deal before others knew what was transpiring." He took possession two hours later, transferring 150 of his men to DeLuxe immediately, since all tools and patterns for the car to be built there had already been prepared in anticipation. About it, LeRoy Pelletier would say only that it would be called the Flanders 20, would have a 100-inch wheelbase, would sell in the $750 range, and would be "a full-sized automobile, not a dinky affair as one might expect at the price indicated." The price was even lower than the Model T, though Henry Ford would soon fix that. A production of 25,000 cars was planned for 1910. Only one-fifth that figure was realized.

Because William Kelly had left the company with his erstwhile partners, Flanders had been forced to come up with a new chief engineer. He settled upon James Heaslet, a self-taught mechanic who had previously bounced around among various small assembled car manufacturers in the field. Heaslet had one good idea and one bad one. The good idea was the multiple uses to which the underframe was put; the motor, magneto, radiator, pump, carburetor, steering gear and dash were all carried on this subframe which consisted of two parallel steel tubes which in turn were supported on cross members secured by four bolts. This simplified manufacture and allowed the low price, and the removal of those four bolts made for a quick and easy lifting of the entire unit from the chassis. This commended itself admirably to commercial application; replacing a unit, which took five minutes at most, meant that

any single car in a fleet could be kept in service at all times. Probably this was considered, but the E-M-F idea was even more ambitious than that. As Pelletier wrote, "We expect this feature to revolutionize present garage practice which necessitates laying up the car for days at a time while some minor repair is being made. In case of any repair or replacement in a Flanders '20,' however serious or simple, the easiest way is to replace the entire unit, send the owner away rejoicing with his car and then, when time best suits and with parts most accessible, make the necessary repair at a minimum of time and expense. The original unit may later be replaced in the car—or if the condition, as to wear, of the two units are about the same the change need not be made—the owner simply charged for time and material in making his unit good." A very interesting notion.

The bad idea Heaslet had was the two-speed transmission; the rear axle just could not bear its strain—the limitations of a two-speed layout of that day are recognized with horror today by antique car buffs—and frequently snapped axles were the result. Consequently the unit was replaced for 1911 by the E-M-F three-speed, and Pelletier insisted that the company admit its mistake and offer to exchange two-speed for three-speed on all the cars in the field. Thereafter he sent the new Flanders on numerous endurance runs—pathfinding for the 1911 Glidden on the East Coast, doing the same on the West Coast for the Pacific Highway Association, and sending a roadster over four-thousand-plus miles from Canada to Mexico—to demonstrate that everything was all right now.

Walter Flanders had said pointedly that this new vehicle was designed for use by

car produced over that number to his workforce "clear down to the office boys and stenographers." When the 1909 World Series was played between the Detroit Tigers and the Chicago White Sox, he declared that if output reached fifty cars a day, half holidays would prevail for everyone so the baseball fans on his team could attend the four games in Detroit. Production records were routinely broken at E-M-F. Sales records were not. This made for a problem. As *The Motor World* explained it, "the E-M-F factory was going full blast and its product was piling up; in due course Mr. Flanders called the Studebakers' attention to the fact."

On December 9th, 1909, Walter Flanders posted a letter to South Bend and at the same time sent it to Detroit daily newspapers and all trade publications to be published as an advertisement. It was a bombshell. In it he declared the alliance with Studebaker as "rescinded and annulled" for a number of reasons, among them the failure of the South Bend people to accept and pay for contracted cars; their unfair discounting of the cars; their advertising which misled readers into believing Studebaker owned a controlling interest in E-M-F, which it did not. Thus was begun what was called the "bitterest legal battle" (*The Automobile*) and the "most engrossing litigation" (*Motor Age*) in the history of the industry thus far.

Noting that no "formal contract signed by both parties" existed indicating it was obliged to take one much less a thousand cars a month—astoundingly, all agreements had been either a handshake or legally non-binding correspondence—Studebaker sought a restraining order and permanent injunction against E-M-F in the U.S. district court in Detroit. This failed, but the company finally managed a temporary injunction from the U.S. circuit court in Cincinnati. In the interim Flanders pushed up production to sixty cars a day and got out a map of the United States. He advertised for dealers, scores of them came rushing to Detroit, Pelletier said he hadn't seen such a stampede since his Klondike days. Circles and squares were made on the map, territories divided up—but this wasn't Flanders' or Pelletier's metier at all. How they wished Bill Metzger was still around.

Studebaker failed to have the temporary injunction made permanent, but that settled nothing. As *Motor Age* noted on January 4th, 1910, the "litigation continues merrily, the past week having seen the inauguration of three new suits, with excellent prospects of a fourth." Walter Flanders traveled to New York in early February to talk to Benjamin Briscoe about possibly amalgamating with United States Motor, but decided against it. A conference was held in South Bend, certainly an unfriendly one, Walter Flanders emerging to state flatly that "we have nothing to gain by a compromise or reconciliation."

What ultimately happened was a takeover. In March it was announced that J.P. Morgan on behalf of Studebaker had purchased sixty-four percent of the stock in E-M-F which, combined with the thirty-six percent acquired in the earlier buying out of Everitt and Metzger, gave South Bend complete control of the company. Particularly emphasized was the fact that Morgan had been acting as broker only and, as *The Horseless Age* noted, "the wild reports that the Napoleon of finance was commencing to form a gigantic $300,000,000 'automobile trust' were quite unfounded . . . thus far Wall Street has not secured a monopoly in the automobile business." A lot of automobile people in Detroit began sleeping easier nights.

Walter Flanders was among them. The entire episode had rattled him, and he saw capitulation in his best interests. Rather like his decision to leave Ford earlier, he believed now that his future with E-M-F was cloudy, he had been irked for some time by the Studebaker practice of having its name typeset larger than his in advertising; it seemed to him that with E-M-F he could never really run his own show. For bowing

the owner "who does not keep a mechanician but looks after his own car"—and to that end LeRoy Pelletier produced one of the most comprehensive and easily understood instruction books of the day. Whether appropriately or not, it assumed the owner knew nothing at all about a motorcar. The manual warned, for example, that a feather duster should not be used on the body ("it will scratch the varnish") nor gasoline to clean the top ("it will dissolve the rubber in the fabric"). Driving hints included: "Your car won't run without gasoline, oil and water. It is a good practice to always make sure yourself that you have these before starting, even on a short trip." And, "when filling the gasoline tank, always extinguish the lamps and be sure your cigar is not lighted." LeRoy didn't miss a thing.

Initially the Flanders 20 was offered in variations on the roadster theme but in March 1911 a foredoor, five-passenger tourer was announced at $800, "the lowest price ever asked for a car with a torpedo type of body." Which it remained until October that year, when Henry Ford lowered his Model T into the $700 range.

Still, the Flanders should have been a lively competitor for the T. The rear axle problem obviously had upset production initially, but it was quickly seen to. Backstage, however, the goings-on were most unpleasant. Walter Flanders was discovering that his friends Barney and Bill had perhaps been right all along about the Studebakers.

At the factory Flanders now had things well in hand, with his friends general superintendent Wollering and factory manager Walburn competently in charge. He had set a thousand-car-a-month production schedule and offered a bonus for every

parts. He accepts the magnificently printed and elaborate catalog as evidence sufficient. . . . Studebakers propose to change all that. We propose to so educate the public that every man considering the purchase of an automobile will insist first on comparing the prices at which replacement parts can be had. . . . The abuses that have prevailed in this industry from the first and up to the time when the Studebakers stepped into this arena are simply incredible." Pelletier was a master.*

Still, his heart was not in all this. Neither was Walter Flanders': With part of his million dollars, the latter bought 1200 acres of farm land surrounding two lakes near Pontiac with the view of transforming it into a plantation, and he created a petty cash fund for taking a number of people out to dinner to talk business. Out of this came—in January 1911—the Flanders Manufacturing Company, a consolidation of the Grant & Wood Manufacturing Company of Chelsea, the Pontiac Motorcycle Company, the Pontiac Drop Forge Company, the Pontiac Foundry Company and the Vulcan Gear Works (also in Pontiac). Capitalized at $2.25 million, most of the money came from former E-M-F backers, Flanders even managing to talk Clement Studebaker, Jr. out of $200,000 in exchange for a seat on the board of directors. Flanders was described as the "moving spirit" of the new company and was a director as well, though the presidency title was given to one of his associates, Robert M. Brownson. The whole object of the consolidation was stated to be the manufacture of the Flanders Bi-Mobile, or two-wheeled automobile. When it arrived later that year it looked like a motorcycle, which it undeniably was—and LeRoy Pelletier, who had thought up the other name, decided that calling a spade a garden implement didn't change its character, and so the $175 Flanders 4 was thereafter termed a motorcycle. Pelletier's involvement was strictly sub rosa at this point, lest his position with Studebaker be endangered.

It was Pelletier, too, who talked Walter into the Flanders Electric. It was announced that summer, priced at $1775, and differed from conventional cars of its type with its adoption of worm drive, cradle spring suspension, a coupé body twelve inches lower than the average ("therefore, less wind resistance"), and anti-friction bearings throughout, combined with a less weighty chassis, to make for easier running, increased mileage on one charge of the battery and better hill climbing. The aim was to "infuse red blood" into the electric field and belie the notion that "parlor prattle and pretty pictures" were the only way to sell an electric carriage, and a refined lady the only customer who would buy one. "Wise and Foolish Statements About Electrics" was the title of the little booklet written by an unnamed "advertising man" and published about this new Flanders. No one in the industry reading it would have had any doubts about its authorship. Doubtless a copy was not sent to South Bend.

Matters quickly became sticky anyway. The manufacture of an electric car and a motorcycle by the Flanders organization did not on the face of it represent a conflict of interest between Flanders himself and his position at Studebaker. But Brownson, after an argument with Flanders, resigned the presidency of Flanders Manufacturing, and at the board of directors meeting that December—not attended, significantly, by Clement Studebaker—who was elected the new president? None other than Walter Flanders. This did not sit well in South Bend. Flanders already had a full-time job at Studebaker. Subsequently, that company created a new position called corporate general manager—Flanders' title being general manager of the

to these realities, he was handsomely rewarded, a million dollars worth for his stock, and he agreed to continue for a term of three years as general manager of Studebaker Corporation which would be formally organized on Valentine's Day, 1911, combining E-M-F and the Studebaker Brothers Manufacturing Company.

For his holdings LeRoy Pelletier received $175,000, in addition to a contract to continue as Studebaker advertising manager at a princely salary of $20,000 a year. James Heaslet formally resigned as E-M-F engineer but was immediately picked up by Studebaker and was soon that company's vice-president of engineering. He and the Studebaker staff refined the cars—beefing up the rear axle still further; this was admittedly the car's weakest point, though it was no more serious a failing than most of its contemporaries suffered in other areas of design—and they were marketed under the E-M-F or Flanders names for 1912, though the type size of the Studebaker logo was now bigger than ever. In 1913 they all became Studebakers.

With his $20,000 a year salary, LeRoy Pelletier found he could write as convincingly for the Studebakers as he had for Walter Flanders. He adroitly promoted the one-two-three victory of the E-M-F in the Tiedeman Trophy race concomitant to the Grand Prize in November 1911. (The E-M-F was an admirable performer, the ninth car produced, nicknamed Old Bullet still held the Atlanta Speedway speed record at over 84 mph.) But he remained best in his getting-down-to-the-facts and leveling-with-the-reader approach on other matters, as in the manipulative price cutting rampant in the industry vis-à-vis the frankly stated competitive business reasons the E-M-F was now $1000: ". . . we never could fathom the philosophy of the ostrich—nor see the sense of treating as trade secrets, matters that were patent to the whole world. You fool nobody but yourself. Besides, it's bad advertising, for it is palpably evasive." Or the price gouging engaged in with regard to replacement parts: "Strange, is it not, then, that not once in a hundred times does the prospective buyer ask for a price list of

352

---

*His spelling and punctuation were atrocious, however—and his proofreading not much better. The writer has on occasion taken the liberty of correction and gentle editing.

"Studebaker Corporation 'automobile interest' "—and filled it with James Newton Gunn (whose older brother was in England, incidentally, building the Lagonda).

For the next two months denials were issued on both sides that Flanders would be leaving Studebaker. But in March he did indeed resign, or try to, there being a logistic difficulty since he was under contract to the company, and this one had been signed. In May there was a reconciliation, though not the one everyone expected.

Walter Flanders announced that he was rejoining his old partners . . . and would now become general manager of the Metzger Motor Car Company which, the reader will remember, was engaged in the building of the Everitt automobile. When asked by reporters if this turn of events might not result in a lawsuit by Studebaker, Flanders replied, "That is quite possible. I believe I am not under contract anymore. I have been given very little to do around the Studebaker plants lately. They claim the right to use my name in the event of my quitting the company. I do not believe they have that right, and this difference of opinion may result in some entanglements."

Rumors followed that the Metzger and Flanders companies would be merged, and recapitalized at $3 million, and the press brought LeRoy Pelletier out of the closet by suggesting he would serve as advertising manager of the new concern. The only thing definite which happened in the next few weeks was the revelation in June that, yes, there was a new company succeeding Metzger, capitalized at $3 million (soon raised

to $3.75), but it was to be called the Everitt Motor Car Company. The absurdity of all this finally prompted Studebaker, in August, to release Flanders from his contract and to allow him to engage in the manufacture of gasoline automobiles which he could call by any name he chose. The next day a press release was issued noting that the Everitt Motor Car Company had changed its name to the Flanders Motor Company.

E and M without F had been rather like pasta without parmesan, something was missing. Everitt knew how to capitalize, Metzger knew how to sell, but neither of them could produce like Flanders. The Metzger Motor Car Company had never really been set up properly. Everitt and Metzger were delighted to have Flanders back—and were amenable to the company name change, realizing Flanders' ego was easily the equal of theirs combined. Flanders stole Fred Hawes away from Cadillac's engineering department—he had been with that company since its inception, Metzger remembered and recommended him. He was not, however, given a whole lot to do. The new Flanders would be the old Everitt, with the addition of Gray & Davis electric lighting and starting, and minor refinements to make production easier.

Sixes only would be marketed, the 127-inch wheelbase 50-Six, and a smaller companion car, the 40-Six on a 115-inch wheelbase. And LeRoy Pelletier got to work. The day of the four was over, he decided, "If You Are Paying More Than $1200 for a Car,

354

You Are Entitled to a Six." Of course, he couldn't promise "to give you a Six at exactly the figure mentioned"—he was writing before Flanders finalized production costs—but he did promise "a price so little above that figure it will be within your reach if you can afford a car of more than 35 horsepower at all." As it happened, the 40-Six came in at $1550—the 50-Six was over two thousand—so Pelletier tried another tack. "Four and Two Do Not Make Six" was the name of the booklet, and it advanced the notion, in Pelletier's inimitable style, that the rush now to the six-cylinder bandwagon by four-cylinder manufacturers was much too hasty: "The obvious way to make a six is to add to the four you already have. . . . But it simply can't be did! . . . The designing of a six is a problem entirely separate from that of designing a four." The new Flanders was introduced, three months later, at the New York Automobile Show, January 1913.

By that time everything had changed—drastically. Firstly, Flanders Manufacturing went into receivership in December 1912. An absolutely scathing news report in *Motor World* suggested the reason was Flanders' "thirst for millions." There was truth in this. An acquaintance had noted that "he asked nothing better than a gambler's chance to play for big stakes"—and he lost. The article went on to lambaste Pelletier as having swayed Flanders unwisely in both the motorcycle and electric car ventures, with time and money frittered away on a $100 Bi-mobile which finally arrived "as a purely conventional machine at a conventional price" and of which, in two years, less than 2500 were built of the thirty or forty thousand planned—and the rush to electric car production which resulted in 3000 orders immediately but also resulted in a machine the bugs of which had not been worked out, the price of which was too low to make a profit, and the production for which totaled something less than a hundred.

Flanders Manufacturing had been an E-M-F—Every Morning Frustration. But the biggest problem apparently was the plant in Chelsea, "a large, imposing structure, originally built on an idealized scale with the funds of the taxpayers of Michigan by a defaulting state official." It included a library, a theatre, a gymnasium, a swimming pool "and other things designed to make the workmen happy" . . . but not the facilities to make them productive. All previous owners hadn't been able to make the factory work; doubtless Flanders, with his experience in such matters, thought he could. He made a mistake. It was a very costly one. Now he found himself, among other debts, unable to pay the contractor who had installed $250,000 worth of improvements to the plantation he had bought with the sellout to Studebaker. Walter Flanders needed cash—badly.

No one ever accused him of not being resourceful. He outdid himself this time. He exchanged one company in receivership for another company in receivership. He broke off ties with Flanders Manufacturing and took on a fiasco someone else had created which was even bigger than his own—Benjamin Briscoe's United States Motor Corporation. (See "The Benjamin Briscoe Story," Volume XVII, Number 2.) In exchange for his services, he required U.S. Motor to purchase the Metzger-Motor-Car-Company-cum-Everitt-Motor-Car-Company-cum-Flanders-Motor-Company. The price was the $3.75 million at which it had only recently been capitalized—a million of that in cash, the rest in stock in the new company to be organized. This made for a nifty profit for investors Everitt and Metzger who merrily went their separate ways, Everitt back to his body-building business which had remained prosperous throughout this saga, Metzger on to affiliations in a number of automotive-related companies including Columbia of Detroit, builders of an assembled car which was among the most respected in this country.

357

Built in September of 1912, and owned today by Leon and Sharon Mills, this Flanders Model 20 had the attractive selling price of just $750.00

Meanwhile Walter Flanders took the remains of U.S. Motor, and having learned a hard lesson, decided retrenchment was sometimes preferable to gambling. At the Knickerbocker Hotel in New York, on two sheets of notepaper, he drafted out the reorganization. He scrapped every sick company in the U.S. Motor colossus, and concentrated on the one healthy organization and the one good name that was left. One month after its introduction at the New York Automobile Show, the Flanders Six became the Maxwell.

And soon thereafter the Flanders Electric became the Tiffany. That was LeRoy Pelletier's doing—and his baby. He would take care of advertising Maxwells for Flanders, both for reasons of friendship and sustenance. But he couldn't get the idea out of his head that there remained a large market for the electric car, if only the right one could be produced. So he teamed up with former Flanders Manufacturing general manager Don McCord, bought what was left of the Flanders Electric business, reintroducing its product as the Tiffany in DeLuxe and Mignon (the latter French of course for tiny or delicate, as in filet). The new name made for catchy phrases—"Of all things She'd like, She'd like a Tiffany best"—but what Pelletier really wanted was a Tiffany with a Woolworth price tag, and this was announced in December 1913: a $750 electric which set an unprecedentedly low price in the electric field . . . but which met the same fate as his $100 motorcycle. He struggled for a while, decided that since a million dollars had been spent promoting the Flanders Electric, its name was perhaps better than one associated only with jewelry, and asked his friend Walter if he'd mind if he switched back. Walter readily agreed, his ego hankering for a car called the Flanders, even though he knew he could pay off his plantation renovations only by producing the Maxwell.

Alas, the Tiffany didn't sell any better as a Flanders this time than it had the first—and ultimately Pelletier concluded he was better off advertising cars other people knew better how to build, like Walter Flanders' Maxwell. Or John Perrin's Lozier or Ransom Olds' Reo. In November of 1914 he established an advertising agency in Detroit. His reputation by now was firmly fixed. In succeeding years he would promote the aeroplane as well—campaigning to make Detroit the air center of the world—and he lent his talents to such "huge amusement enterprises" as Luna Park, Coney Island and Madison Square Garden. He would be generally credited with introduction of the "Midway" concept into expositions and world fairs.

Which brings us, by quantum jump, to 1921. When Barney Everitt picked up the phone to say hi to his old partners and ask if they'd like to join him in a new car-building venture he was contemplating with Eddie Rickenbacker. William Metzger was dubious—he was enjoying a leisurely seat on numerous boards of directors and was about to assume the Michigan distributorship for the Wills-Sainte-Claire, but for the sake of friendship of course he'd help any way he could. Walter Flanders was dubious too; he'd made a success of Maxwell and was now enjoying retirement as a gentleman farmer, but for the sake of friendship, of course. . . . E and M and F were back together again. And they all called LeRoy. Pelletier said sure. It was a reunion. It was a comeback.

The Rickenbacker, unfortunately, like the E-M-F, suffered callously unfair jibes from its competitors (these because of its early introduction of four-wheel brakes, the complete story is told in "Hat in the Ring: The Rickenbacker," Volume XIII, Number 4). It lived only a half decade, a year longer than the E-M-F. It was the last automotive venture for Everitt, Metzger and Flanders.

One is left with the nagging suspicion that, from the beginning, things might have been different had these people just been able to stay together long enough.

On June 16th, 1923, at age fifty-two, Walter Flanders died from injuries suffered in an automobile crash three weeks earlier. The impact of his death on the ultimate fate of the Rickenbacker, although unmeasurable, was very real. Obituary writers for the Detroit newspapers noted his having been married three times. Two further marriages had slipped by them. A month later three of his ex-wives—his second wife had died—contested his will, alleging they had been disinherited from the $1.5 million estate because of pressures brought to bear on Flanders by wife number five. Four of his five children—one from his second marriage, three from his fourth—had also been cut out of the will, and they joined in the suit. It was an unseemly business, ultimately settled privately.

On April 11th, 1933, William E. Metzger died, age sixty-four, at his home in Detroit. It was a blessing, the press said, he had been incapacitated for four years, "critically ill for the past year, and in recent months had suffered a weakening of the mind." A heart attack released him. His wife had died in 1907, his daughter survived him.

On September 5th, 1938, heart disease claimed LeRoy Pelletier at the age of seventy. For years, in memory of his friend Elbert Hubbard who liked them, he had worn only Windsor ties, though he had to go to children's departments to buy them. He had asked his wife to bring one along when he checked into Henry Ford Hospital in Detroit. Two sons, a daughter, a brother and eight grandchildren also survived him.

On October 5th, 1940, in Harper Hospital in Detroit, with his wife, his brother and sister at his bedside, Barney Everitt died at age sixty-seven. He had been in failing health for more than a year.

Risking sacrilege, it might be conjectured that now they're all back together again, finishing what they only hesitatingly began a few times before. Somewhere up there a mighty comeback is being staged. Maybe this one will be called the E-M-F-P . . . or M-E-F-P . . . or F-M-E-P . . . or . . . LeRoy always did deserve billing.✥

"Built by Studebaker, Detroit, Mich.," the radiator emblem says, but the 1912 demi-tonneau (left) is an E-M-F, owned by John S. Carroll.   Studebaker claimed the roadster (above) as well, but it's a 1912 Flanders Model 20, and from the collection of the Discovery Hall Museum.

The cable read: "George Merwin, Hotel Duville, Monza, Italy. Proceed to Monte Carlo. Meet Tom Tierney at Hotel de Paris. He has all details. Regards Passino, Dearborn, Michigan, USA."

As I looked around at my roommates of the past three days, Colin Chapman, Jimmy Clark and Gerald "Gaby" Crombec—publisher of the popular French magazine *Sport Auto*—I remarked that it looked like a decision had finally been made to rally the Ford Falcon. We had just returned to the hotel from a losing Lotus effort in the Italian Grand Prix and Colin and Jimmy were packing to fly to England. Said Clark, "If you get a rally team going, I might be interested in taking a ride. I understand it can be a bit of fun."

At that, Chapman snapped back, "There'll be no rally car rides for you as long as you're under contract to me. Rally driving is a damn good way to get yourself killed."

"Gentlemen," I interjected, "you have me at a disadvantage. I don't know the first thing about international rallies."

"That gives you the advantage of not having any bad habits to get rid of," said Chapman.

Colin's statement, while seemingly made in jest, helped somewhat to quell the queasiness in my stomach as I packed to head for Monte Carlo. I had just observed my first Grand Prix race as a prelude to the Ford/Lotus Indianapolis effort and was apparently about to get involved in something else which would be new to me. I had previously heard inklings and rumors about rallying bandied about between our ad agency, J. Walter Thompson, and our marketing,

public relations and performance management. But I was not privy to those meetings as I was in the field seeing that our various performance programs were happening as my boss, Jacque Passino, expected them to happen. Thus I was fortunate to participate in a run from Miami to New York in a Ford-powered speedboat that broke Gar Wood's thirty-year-old record. Then, after the boat finished second in the 1962 London *Daily Express* Ocean Power Boat Race, I was sent to evaluate the Lotus Car Company and its ability to design and build a racing car to compete in the 1963 Indy 500. That was how I came to be at Monza.

Gaby Crombec accompanied me partway to Monte Carlo and filled me in on some of the unique situations I would encounter in European-type rallying versus our American "mathematical calculator" type. He became one of our staunchest supporters and did much to publicize our efforts while helping to explain our side of any verbal confrontation with various European competitors and the sometimes anti-American press.

At Ford, I was brought up to date on plans by Tom Tierney, top PR creative light and number two man to PR boss, Walter Murphy. We were to introduce the V-8-powered 1963½ Falcon Sprint in Monte Carlo just prior to the start of the Monte Carlo Rally in January 1963. To highlight the announcement, we would fly a hundred top automotive writers over to help us explain to the American public the rally's importance as a test of a car's handling and durability. Tierney told me that my part in the operation was simple. He read from an assignment of responsibilities sheet:

"George Merwin will put together a team to participate in the Monte Carlo Rally with the objective

of competing well enough to be able to produce favorable publicity, promotion and advertising to inject some excitement into the somewhat stodgy image the public has of the present Falcon."

After the meeting with Tom Tierney, I laid my plans quickly and carefully. I set up three meetings for the following day in three different countries, realizing I was about to have one of the busiest days of my life. It began with breakfast with Robert Sobra, secretary of the Automobile Club of Monaco. We discussed the rules and regulations for participation in the 1963 Monte Carlo Rally. The organizers were anxious to have us participate and would assist us in every possible way, wanting the good publicity.

As I reflect back, I don't think they felt that a large American car—even the Falcon was considered large—had much of a chance on the narrow winding, mountainous roads which made up much of the route. So obviously they weren't too worried about upsetting regular competitors by promoting our entry. After my breakfast meeting, I was loaded down with entry blanks and the latest rule books and hustled aboard a plane for Paris for a luncheon with Bill Reiber, president of Ford of France and his PR director and performance manager, André Chemin. We discussed drivers, mechanics, possible tie-ins and any role that the French Ford company might play in assisting us in the venture.

Third meeting and third country. I had dinner at the Steering Wheel Club in London with Sid Henson, competition manager for Ford of England. When I told him of my plans for putting together a rally team, he sort of smiled. When I added that we would also have

OF FORDS AND FINNS
The Monte Carlo Rally and the Falcon Sprint

to make a creditable showing, he laughed out loud. He pointed out that I was being asked to do the impossible in trying to assemble a first-class rally operation in such a short space of time. First and foremost, all the top drivers were under contract already and secondly, we proposed to run a vehicle that had never been tested or even been driven over European rally routes at speed. I thanked him for his concern but told him that what I needed now was his counsel and recommendations. He agreed to help. By the end of the following week, I had a team manager, Jeff Uren.

Jeff was a former Ford of England competition manager and a meticulous organizer. We immediately began the task of sorting out qualifications of available drivers. Both Jeff and Sid were high on a Swedish ice racing champion named Bosse Ljungfeldt. Bo was a monster of a man with great strength, a ready smile and a love of competition. He was already under contract to Ford of England to drive a Cortina in the Swedish Midnite Sun Rally but wasn't considered necessary for the already strong Ford Monte team.

A quick phone call to Stockholm to Ford of Sweden's competition chief, Gillis Lof—a close friend of Bo's—got us a positive reaction. Bosse spoke very little English but understood it fairly well. Gillis called him and got back to us the same day. Bosse agreed to drive and Gunnar Haggbom would navigate. We considered getting Haggbom a real coup as he had been the navigator in the 1962 winning Saab with Erik Carlsson: He was also a perfect foil for the taciturn Ljungfeldt and his English was impeccable.

We next picked Peter Jobb, a Britisher with some

by George F. Merwin

with a painting by Walter Gotschke

background in amateur motor racing and rallying. This also gave us an opportunity to use Trant Jarman, then the American Midwest sales manager for *Car and Driver*, who had competed in several Canadian rallies which were the closest thing to a European rally you could find in North America.

For our third team, we were able to get Britisher Anne Hall, a woman with some of the best credentials in rally sport including the top women's prize in the Alpine Rally. Anne was also a regular on Ford of Britain's East African Safari team. Her navigator was a Scottish lass named Margaret McKensie. Now our group was complete except for one major exception—support drivers and mechanics.

I met with Walter Hays, the new public affairs director for Ford of England and laid out my plans. He recommended that I work out a deal with Bob Scruton, managing director of Lincoln Cars Ltd., for work space and mechanics. Lincoln Cars Ltd. was a Ford subsidiary responsible for importing all Ford products built outside England. This, of course, meant that the company's mechanics were familiar with American-built Fords.

With three months to go, Jeff Uren and I headed for Dearborn. We first met with John Holman, president of Holman and Moody, builders of our winning Ford stock cars. Jeff told John what he needed in the Falcon to make it a finisher and even a possible contender for top honors. The car would be based on the new Falcon Sprint with a 260-cubic-inch V-8 fitted with Cobra modifications to bring power from l64 to 260 hp. The car was also to be fitted with front disc brakes and such suspension modifications as revised pitman and idler arms, an extra rear spring leaf to reduce axle wind-up, Koni shocks and a Galaxie limited-slip rear with 4.5l gears. Those special pieces would, of course, have to be included in the car's homologation papers.

There was that word again—homologation. At first, it had sounded kind of obscene to me but I soon learned it meant we would have to build a thousand basic units as described in our papers plus any additional parts as specified within the rules of the category in which we planned to compete. We were very busy. We had to build three practice cars and get a mountain of spare parts shipped to Lincoln Cars Ltd. in London. The cars had to be prepped there and made ready for their crews who needed to practice in them over the various special speed stages. Our drivers needed more practice than the others because they were completely

unfamiliar with the Ford Falcon. Anne Hall's first comment upon driving one was that it felt like a "bloody lorry." While practice was progressing late in November, we were completing the actual rally cars in Charlotte, North Carolina at Holman and Moody and our homologation papers were submitted for approval. Jeff Uren completed the team by hiring several former race and rally drivers to pilot our support vehicles. Veteran British driver, Sam Croft-Pearson was hired to head the service crews which included drivers Paul Hawkins and two former winners of the East African Safari, John Manussis and Bill Fritschy. An elaborate service operation was planned with cars criss-crossing the rally route to ensure that at any given time during the rally, no service automobile was ever too far away from a car that might need help. This, of course, was over and above each service vehicle's assignment at each of the twenty-five official checkpoints.

During the practice sessions, John Holman and I decided to join Jeff Uren and get some first-hand experience in what European rally driving was all about. We spent one whole night in and out of a little restaurant and hotel at the base of Europe's famous hill climb site, Mt. Ventoux, in the village of Bedoin. On that very cold and very dark night, I had three of the most memorable rides in a career which has

encompassed a lot of wild rides on land, sea and air.

I rode with Bosse and Gunnar. I was in the back seat with the rest of the spare parts. The ride is a little hazy in my mind since once Bosse pointed the car down the road, you sort of went into a state of shock. It was a euphoria similar to accounts I've read of drug trips. Nothing appeared real. You knew wild things were going on but that nothing could disturb you. You heard Gunnar directing Bosse right or left through the fog as he deciphered his pace notes. Bosse acknowledged with a gutteral "ugh" or something spicier in Swedish when he missed a gear as he constantly shifted up and down through the Falcon's close ratio box, striving to get maximum speed on glare ice while throwing the car hard right and hard left until the summit was reached. A quick check of Gunnar's stopwatch, a grunt from Bosse and we hurtled back down the mountain to try to knock a few hundredths of a second off on the next attempt. That's how you become the fastest car on the hill. After the hair-raising ride up, I thought we would have a leisurely trip down. Then I learned that leisurely was not a word in Bosse's vocabulary.

I might add that Bosse drove like this on a totally impossible road. My own car, a Fairlane sedan without spiked tires, was unable to reach the top. You haven't

A Falcon Squire for the Monaco Red Cross: Mr. and Mrs. Benson Ford present the car to Princess Grace.

lived until you find yourself sliding backwards down a twisty mountain road in pitch dark fog on glare ice. By fitting chains, we were able to continue.

During the various practice sessions I noticed how, on a crew's first run over a special timed speed section, the driver would go slowly to allow the navigator to make his "pace" notes. As they proceeded, the navigator wrote what the road did and marked distances on his pace chart. For example, he might write: "...hard left...straight five kilometers easy left...hard right, hard left...long sloping right...long straight 10 kilometers then very long left...sharp right," etc. They then tested the notes at speed and made corrections. The driver and navigator literally bet their lives on the notes' accuracy, especially since most special speed stages were run at night in the Maritime Alps. The weather is usually bad with ice and fog. You can't see more than a few feet ahead of the car as you drive upwards of 100 to 130 mph.

After piling up many gruelling miles, the practice cars were returned to London and the knowledge gained led to further suspension modifications and lighting changes. Each car was now equipped with two flame throwers which illuminated the road in nearly all weather and two brilliant fog lamps to cut through the

inevitable fog, snow, rain and sleet during those long, dark nights. These were, of course, in addition to the headlights. One of the flame throwers was mounted on the roof for the co-driver to control and he could move its beam from side to side as the car swung left and then right in and out of sharp corners in which the car would frequently be sideways.

A multitude of spare parts was carried in the car's back seat, tied down with shock cords. Special spiked tires were the last important additions. Ljungfeldt arranged to have tungsten steel spikes added to tires in Finland, giving the Falcon excellent control on ice at top speeds. Each tire contained 672 spikes and Bosse, with his incredible ability, could drive on glare ice as fast as dry pavement.

We were now as ready as we would ever be. We proceeded to Monte Carlo to the local Ford dealer, Auto Riviera, for the final tuning of our three Falcons. My bosses and all the invited automotive writers arrived and the pre-Monte activities got under way. Princess Grace accepted a new Falcon Squire on behalf of the Monaco Red Cross and the auto writers took part in a special rally for the press. The Principality was thronged by tourists anxious to see some of the special rally cars.

I had decided it would be nice if Ford management

got a first-hand impression of what the Monte Carlo Rally was all about and arranged for my boss, Jacque Passino, to ride with Anne Hall and Margaret McKensie. Marketing boss E.F. "Gar" Laux went for a ride with Peter Jopp and Trant Jarman, and Ford Division chief Lee Iacocca went off with Bosse and Gunnar. That evening when I again saw Iacocca, I was greeted with, "Merwin... you're fired!" I smiled. I knew he was joking but the only thing was that he wasn't smiling. He turned away to talk to a group of writers.

I really didn't enjoy my lunch because Iacocca didn't look at me all through the various courses. It wasn't until his talk following the different award presentations that I could begin breathing again. He mentioned that he had ridden with our Swedish team and he had gone into shock as they threaded their way through the many curves and hairpins up and down the mountains. He mentioned that when the ride was over, Gunnar told him that Bosse didn't drive fast in deference to Iacocca's position with Ford. But Bosse's idea of slow was unreal. Iacocca mentioned that he had fired me but that I could redeem myself by ensuring a good performance in the Monte. He was smiling as he said it.

After the press contingent departed Monaco, we got ready for the start. There were eight starting points

Prince Rainier (center) learns about the '63 Falcon rally car from George Merwin. Benson Ford is at the left. Behind Merwin is Ford's Walter Murphy.   Ljungfeldt's Falcon in action.

The way to victory: Carlsson flings his Saab through the streets of Monte Carlo to conclude the '63 rally. Below: Scrutineering for the '63 Shell 4000 in Canada. Opposite: Practicing in the Canadian Rockies outside Vancouver.

available in the 1963 Monte Carlo Rally: Glasgow, Stockholm, Paris, Warsaw, Athens, Monte Carlo, Frankfurt and Lisbon. The cars would then drive various routes until they all wound up in Chambery, France, where they would take a common route to Monte Carlo. We started at Monte Carlo despite the protests of our Swedish team who wanted Stockholm. I had agreed but was overruled by management who wanted as much tie-in as possible with Monte Carlo. As it turned out, we might have picked up all the marbles if we had started in Stockholm.

Right after an uneventful start on a beautiful, sunny day, the weather turned bad. Snow started to fall and fall and fall. It reminded me of a northern Michigan blizzard and it quickly began to pile up heavily in the Maritime Alps. The snow covered over icy spots and Bosse found himself making an unexpected excursion off the road in a fast corner. Luckily, with a little help from one of our service cars, he was able to get going again without too much loss of time. Then all the cars which had started at Monte Carlo got bogged down near the town of Lodeve. All three Falcons were trapped behind other cars.

Ljungfeldt changed to his spikes and, after helping some of the smaller cars in front through the pass, he was able to proceed and Jopp followed. Anne Hall, however, elected to join some other cars trying to find an alternate route. It proved almost nonexistent and she came to the checkpoint completely out of time and was eliminated from the rally. Bosse and Peter arrived at the checkpoint with points against them for being late and Bosse lost even more time when he had to repair his clutch.

Meanwhile, John Holman and I decided to see what conditions were like for ourselves and, after a last look at a big wall map with the rally route marked out, we embarked for Chambery. The roads were terrible and our Fairlane with its regular tires slid all over the road. We soon became lost and stopped by a snow-covered sign to study our Michelin map. When I got out of the car to have a closer look at the sign, I immediately slipped and slid under the car. As I tried to lift myself up by grabbing the driver's seat through the open door, I actually pulled the whole car sideways. That's slippery! When we finally reached one of our service points at a special stage, I literally commandeered a set of spike tires.

From Chambery to Monaco the real rally started, for Chambery is where the special stages begin. By now all the Athens starters were snowed in somewhere in

Yugoslavia and all the Lisbon starters were out. Roads were covered with packed snow and glare ice and visibility was zero. There were six special all-out speed stages covering some ninety of the toughest miles in Europe. Bosse won all six. Even with the handicap system imposed on his larger engine. This was the first time that one car had won on all the special stages.

Despite this, the overall placement of the two finishing Falcons was low, Jopp/Jarman placed thirty-fifth, Ljungfeldt/Haggbom forty-third. Erik Carlsson in his 850 cc Saab won for the second straight year, followed by a Citroën, a Mini, and two more Citroëns. We, however, had accomplished more than we dreamed possible. With Bosse's fantastic feat, we could talk superior speed. With two of our three cars finishing, we could talk durability. With Jopp/Jarman placing first in the over 3000 cc category, we had a class win to trumpet. J. Walter Thompson did such a good job exploiting all this that Saab had to retaliate with ads pointing out that "only one car won the Monte Carlo."

With the Monte over, we arranged to loan a rally car to Ford of France for its rally program and shipped the Jopp/Jarman car to the United States for inclusion in the Ford display at the Chicago auto show. When I returned to Dearborn late in January, I was asked to furnish three Falcon Sprints to Ford of Canada for the Shell 4000, and we had the cars prepared at Dearborn Steel Tubing Company which did a lot of Ford's prototype and show car work. Dearborn Steel had a lot of enthusiastic young mechanics and also attracted many up-and-coming Ford engineers who moonlighted there to have some fun. The Falcons won a class prize in the prestigious Canadian rally.

Back in Europe, Anne Hall and Margaret McKensie took an outright win in Holland's Tulip Rally. Henri Chemin, Ford of France's racing boss, was so elated when he described the win to me over the phone from Paris that I finally had to holler, "Whoa." He was talking very fast French and I hadn't the slightest idea of what he said after he first opened with, "Hello George. This is Henri. I have fantastic news." The rest was French.

After the Shell 4000 and the Falcon's Tulip Rally win, I was asked to prepare a program for the balance of 1963 and a proposal for 1964 through mid-year when we would have an all-new car. We called it T5. It would be introduced as the Mustang, but that's a whole story in itself. For the balance of '63, I proposed we enter a car in the Swedish Midnite Sun Rally in June, the

Alpine Rally in July and the Liège-Sofia-Liège Rally, the latter with an all-out Group 4 car. Our final rally of 1963 would be the RAC in November. For 1964, we would hit the Monte with an eight-car team, the Shell 4000 with two cars in addition to three Canadian Falcons, a single entry in the Midnite Sun Rally and three cars for the Alpine.

Not all of these plans went smoothly. When I arrived in Sweden to prepare for the Midnite Sun Rally, I found that I was as welcome as a bad case of the flu. Ford of Sweden didn't import the Falcon; Ljungfeldt was committed to drive a Cortina which was imported and,

after finally signing up a local driver named Bjarne Lundberg, our car was eliminated early in the rally after an accident with a truck. In the Alpine Rally, several speed stages were won as well as a class victory. But the Liège-Sofia-Liège Rally proved to be brutal. The organizers of the event advised us proudly that only ten cars had finished the previous year and they hoped fewer would finish this year! They had one other idiosyncracy; they refused to accept any protests at all.

The following cable summed up our Liège experience perfectly: "No Falcons finished. Mechanical all three. Basically suspension. Worst roads in world coupled with torrential rains made for horrible conditions. Twenty cars of one hundred thirty-five finished. All cars had penalties. First five places' Mercedes 230 SL - Saab - Citroën - Cortina - Citroën. All Group Four special built cars. It is apparent that Falcon in present form is not Liège material. Falcon chassis engineers must collaborate with Holman Moody on complete new suspension and front end. With work started now and much testing we could have excellent chance next year. This is Mercedes third overall win. Their first year they did not finish. Will call you later in week."

We did manage to win the Geneva Rally in Switzerland but the popular RAC, with 400 miles of special stages on private forestry roads, war department test areas and various race tracks, was unsuccessful for us. Our cars dropped out one-two-three with Ljungfeldt being the last to disappear into the slop that was a forestry division quagmire of mud called a road in northern Scotland.

While these rallies were all taking place, I had been darting back and forth across the Atlantic like a yo-yo, thirty-eight round trips in 1963. After hiring Alan Mann to oversee our cars' preparation in England, we formalized plans for 1964. We planned to enter an eight-car team in the Monte using the new 1964 Falcon Rally Sprint as a basis. The car would be made lighter than the previous model thanks to fiberglass door and hood panels. We also took advantage of its new 289-cubic-inch engine to boost horsepower to 305. Alan and I went to Dearborn and sat down with our parts people and ordered sufficient spares for the eight rally cars plus more for eight practice cars. We arranged with Holman and Moody to prepare seven Econoline vans for support vehicles. These were equipped with 427 engines, bigger axles and wheels and the same rear end that went into our NASCAR cars. After testing, the vans were dubbed "The Beasts." Holman said grinning, "If the Falcons don't go quick enough, sneak in one of these."

We hired a formidable team for the Ford assault on the 1964 Monte Carlo Rally. Starting from Oslo would be Bosse Ljungfeldt and Fergus Sager, Bjarne Lundberg and Berti Rehnfelt, Henri Greder and Marlial Delalande, Jo Schlesser and Claude Leguezac. From Paris: Anne Hall and Denise McCluggage, Peter Jopp and Alain Bertaut, Graham Hill and Ian Walker, Peter Harper and John Sprinzel. During December, each of these teams put in hundreds of practice miles.

Toward the end of that month, I had a chance to talk

At Lincoln Cars Ltd. in London, Falcons undergo preparation for the 1964 Monte Carlo Rally.

to Graham to ask him how everything was going. He remarked about the sheer power of the Falcon but his most enthusiastic comments were reserved for discussing Ljungfeldt's exploits. He told about following Bosse over a special stage on which Bosse actually would pass cars by flinging his Falcon up the face of the mountain bordering the narrow road and then dropping back down. As Graham said, "I saw him do it time after time and I still don't believe it."

Just before Christmas, the seven vans were ready to be shipped to England. We had to fly them over, which took up a lot of space on Pan Am's 707 freighters. So they stuffed our vans with the Christmas packages being sent to American servicemen overseas. One of these vans was fated to become involved in a most trying experience while loaded up with tires and leaving London.

Alan had one of his former race driver friends, who shall remain nameless, drive it to France. While negotiating Trafalgar Square, the busiest intersection in

London, at 5:00 p.m., the chains holding some of the tires in place let go. We were later told that it was a sight to behold. Wheels were flying in every direction, bouncing across the hoods of cars, bouncing up onto roofs and then along the crowded sidewalks. While all this was going on, the traffic cops were jumping up and down and the biggest traffic jam in Trafalgar Square history just kept getting bigger. Through some divine miracle, no one was injured but the BBC gave us a lot of unwanted coverage.

I spent that Christmas at home with my wife and three daughters. The visit was a brief one but there was the welcome promise from Lee Iacocca that he would send my wife to be with me in Monte Carlo. Back in Europe, final routes were marked out for our service vans and final preparations made to the rally cars. Once all the cars and vans had been shipped off to their designated departure sites, Alan and I prepared to leave for Oslo with all the entry papers and documents which would permit us to run the rally.

Bosse Ljungfeldt in a 1964 Monte practice car. Denise McCluggage and Anne Hall discuss strategy and routes. Graham Hill and Ian Walker were also part of the Ford contingent for the '64 event.

We got fogged in! This was one of those London fogs that goes into the history books. From the second floor of the International Building at Heathrow airport, we couldn't see the ground. Nothing was taking off or arriving and we were getting desperate. If our cars didn't start the rally, I knew I would be fired. It was just that simple. Pan Am had one flight on the ground. It was headed for New York. I booked two seats to New York plus two from New York to Oslo. It was a long way around but...Fortunately, a Finnair flight arrived from Helsinki and prepared to return. We rushed over and got two seats to Gothenburg, Sweden where we could change for Oslo.

Just before we left for Oslo, we got word that Chrysler of America was going to field a three-car team of Valiants in the GT category where there was little competition. We immediately switched the Hall/McCluggage and Jopp/Bertaut cars to GT. After taking care of formalities in Oslo and Paris, Alan and I flew to Monte Carlo where we set up our headquarters

in a suite at the Hermitage Hotel. The first message we received was that one of Alan's race driver friends driving a van (Sir John Whitmore, I think) had got upside down. Parts had flown around making things a real shambles but none of the three occupants had been hurt.

There were a total of 299 starters from nine starting points that, besides Paris and Oslo, included Warsaw, Minsk, Frankfurt, Lisbon, Glasgow, Athens and Monte Carlo. The weather was exceptionally dry leaving the initial 2000 or so miles uneventful. Prior to arriving at Rheims, however, Graham Hill had a couple of shunts which required a jury rigged suspension and slowed him down. Rheims will be remembered for more than champagne to many of that year's rally crews. Apparently there was some bad food served and many suffered the last 500 miles of the toughest road sections with "Montezuma's Revenge."

The weather, however, remained fine. Thanks to a cousin of John Holman's who was an Air Force officer,

we had first-hand access to the latest forecasts and we were always able to drop the correct tires at each service point. Bosse turned in some fabulous runs, placing first on four of the special stages and tying for first on the fifth with Paddy Hopkirk's Mini Cooper S. Bosse also set the fastest time over the Monaco Grand Prix course at the rally's end—5 minutes 50.5 seconds, compared to Hopkirk's 6 minutes 24 seconds—amazing everyone except perhaps for himself. This extraordinary single lap helped Bosse take second place overall in an event where the handicap always seemed to me to favor the small displacement cars manufactured in Europe rather than something like the Falcon. Hopkirk placed first. Erik Carlsson's red Saab finished third, nosed out of second by Ljungfeldt's miraculous lap time. The Mini of Timo Makinen/P. Vanson placed fourth, the Saab of Pat Moss Carlsson/Ursula Wirth placed fifth. In addition to Bosse's fine showing, Falcons also finished first and second—Hall/McCluggage and Jopp/Bertaut—in the

367

Rally headquarters: Alan Mann, George Merwin, Judith Jopp. European graffiti. The winning Mini. Above right: A Falcon practices on the narrow road to Nice. Page opposite: The fruits of skill and speed. Ljungfeldt and his navigator, Fergus Sager, at the post-rally ceremony.

over 2500 cc GT class, beating the Valiants, and Ljungfeldt won the over 2500 cc general class. All our cars had finished.

We knew we had now gotten the most we could expect out of the Monte and we advised the organizers that, since their coefficients were so manipulated as to make it impossible for us to improve our results, we would not be returning. To this day, we have kept our word. The following year, they tried to entice us back saying they would throw out the coefficient, but we were then refocusing our performance objectives on other areas. After the 1964 Monte, we started backing off the Falcon effort. The Mustang was on the horizon.

Still, we had commitments to honor. Ljungfeldt and Anne Hall each drove the Shell 4000 and walked off with many of the special stage awards. Bosse wanted to drive the '64 Midnite Sun Rally in front of the "home folks" and we furnished him a car which he drove to fourth overall and a class win. Our final Falcon effort was to be the Alpine Rally, however, events foiled us.

After the Monte, we had been advised by the FIA that we had been protested by the German representative on the committee and that until we could prove our entries were legal under the rules, all our international wins would be withdrawn. I was immediately summoned home from Europe to prepare our rebuttal. In some areas, it became a matter of American interpretation versus French or German. We were exonerated but not in time to save our entries in the Alpine where our cars were removed from the rally just as they were about to begin. All our efforts to reinstate them were fruitless. When I called Jacque Passino to tell him the news, he said: "It's a damn shame for the drivers but probably a blessing for us.

You and Alan get back over here; the Mustang's ready to go."

It was an inauspicious end for a plucky rally car, a car that quickly became nearly forgotten amid the excitement generated by the Mustang. The Falcon was always an also-ran as a youthful performance car. It had been introduced in 1960 as a compact economy car and by the end of 1961 was selling at an annual rate of 493,000 units. But by the end of 1962, annual sales totaled 358,000 and surveys showed lukewarm response from the younger buyer, from the youth market.

We needed some pizzaz for the Falcon without the cost of a complete development program, since the Mustang was to be our weapon for an offensive into the youth market. Thus was born the Falcon Sprint with its 260 V-8, four-speed transmission, and improved

suspension. With the help of our first Monte effort, the Sprint did capture a small segment of the market and helped keep Falcon sales from a really disastrous decline. It was quite a pleasant car, capable of twelve-second 0-60 times—the rally car did sixty in 7.5 seconds—and decent handling. Like many sports oriented cars today, the Sprint could have been the basis for a really outstanding automobile, given some owner modifications. Said Car and Driver in 1963: "A man driving a Sprint with Koni shocks, faster steering, good tires and disc brakes is going to have an awful lot of fun and show a clean pair of heels to a lot of expensive iron." The unmodified car, said the magazine, "can certainly qualify as a fine sports sedan, in the manner of a 3.8 Jag."

None of this kept Falcon sales from slipping even lower. In 1964, 281,000 were sold; only the Sprint kept

this figure from being even worse. The car itself had little lasting impact. It is quite rare today. As for those hairy rally versions, none seem to have survived. It all leaves one wondering what the production Sprint might have become had the whole program not been discontinued.

If there is one person to be singled out as most important to the Falcon rally program, it would have to be Bosse Ljungfeldt who established an instant rapport with the Falcon. He was the only man I ever met who drank scotch and coke and the only man really able to get the full measure of performance from our rally car. With the Falcon, Ljungfeldt shook the very foundations of the European rally establishment. After a particularly good practice run, he would return to us, fling the door almost off its hinges and shout, "Gut car, Yorge," with a smile that lit up the landscape. ✣

369

Preceding pages: Rivals at the Col de Turini. Ljungfeldt slides through a snowy turn on opposite lock as Carlsson's little Saab howls up behind.

Ford's fanciest Falcon. The Sprint with its V-8 power was introduced in 1963. This well-preserved hardtop is owned by Fred and Sandy Dering.

1963 Falcon Sprint convertible • Owner: David Stockton

1964 Falcon Sprint convertible ● *Owner: Sam Clay*

THE STORY OF #471
BUGATTI'S OWN BUGATTI

In 1910 Ettore Bugatti, age twenty-eight, resigned his position at the Deutz Works in Cologne, Germany, determined at last to establish his own carmaking company. He moved from Cologne to Alsace where, in a rented former dye works at Molsheim, he began making automobiles. His plans were well advanced before the move, and by the time he left Deutz, he had already made one prototype of the car he intended to produce. This was the 1208 cc Type 10, the first Pur Sang Bugatti, built in his basement workshop at Cologne, which in production form became the 1327 cc Type 13, the only production model before World War 1.

He also brought with him from Cologne another much more powerful car, a five-liter overhead valve design with three valves per cylinder and chain drive. Bugatti later told Colonel Giles of the Bugatti Owners Club that he had built this car in 1908. The history of the little Type 10 is well known, since it stayed in the Bugatti family until after the Second World War and was purchased eventually by Bill Harrah. The five-liter appeared once, in the 1910 Prince Henry Trial, with Bugatti driving, and then disappeared.

Or did it disappear? It now seems fairly certain that this car was really only half-completed at the time of the 1910 Prince Henry Trial, and that it did not appear in public in its final form for another two years. It was Bugatti's own competition car, not intended for production and it had to wait for a while until the company was on its feet before it could be developed.

In 1912 Bugatti drove a chain-drive five-liter

By Nigel Arnold-Forster
Color Photography by Neill Bruce

Left: Ettore Bugatti poses with a smile behind the wheel of a Deutz built to his own design and driven by him in the 1909 Prince Henry Trials. Chassis 471 at Mont Ventoux in 1912. Two years later, it was owned by the pipe-smoking Duke of Bavaria. Above: Bugatti in 471 at Le Mans in 1912, the car fitted with a nose cowl. Below: Jean and L'Ebé Bugatti dwarfed by their father's racing car. Right: 471 rebodied with Bruno Martinelli at the wheel, circa 1925. Chassis 714 with Friedrich in the car, Bugatti on the horse. 716 posed at Indy, 1915.

racing car at Le Mans and later at the Mont Ventoux hill climb where he finished in fourth place. Recent evidence seems to show that this was the same car which Bugatti had designed in 1908, and partly completed by 1910 in time for the Trial. The evidence is in the form of photographs of the Prince Henry car's engine, published in the Motor magazine in 1911 but wrongly captioned as the Type 13. Not only do these photos clearly show an engine identical to that of the 1912 car, but it is also clear that the engine was not designed for the chassis frame and body to which it was then fitted. The engine had been lifted up on extension plates some four inches to line up with a different transmission, radiator and firewall than Bugatti planned. These components appear to be the same as the ones fitted to the 1912 car and were clearly designed for its rounded body, not the rectangular one fitted to the 1910 machine. For that car, an awkwardly-shaped hood had been made up to transfer the shape from cowl to body. The chassis frame and body of that car appear to be pure Deutz.

So it seems that Bugatti's own racing car in 1912 was not only the car he had designed in 1908 but that as much of it as had been completed by 1910 was used in the Prince Henry Trials version that year. I am now privileged to own this car, and to me the most astonishing thing is the sheer performance of it. My friend Sandy Skinner drove the car recently and wrote this description of his experience in the Bugatti Owners Club journal, Bugantics: "The view from the bridge encompasses a whole lot of bonnet, what appear to be vast wheels, and just two rather marine-looking gauges. One tells you that oil is going round, and the other that fuel can be expected to appear at the carb. There is nothing to indicate the speed of either the engine or the bolide.

"Gear positions are conventional modern, with first and third forward. There is the expected clunk as first goes in; changes on the move are exceptionally easy. Handbrake off, and open the throttle slightly on a steep upgrade from the garage. The throttle turns out to be higher geared than expected. The result is that you get hit in the back hard enough to hurt. The car takes off in the way one would expect from a well set up lightweight V-8.

"A brisk trot up a very Prescott-like hill showed why the car massacred the Edwardian record at Shelsley, and came close to the Prescott record in streaming rain—beating it unofficially in practice. It is enormously tweakable, which probably makes it a better sprint than circuit machine, and goes exactly where it is pointed. The torque at low revs continues, seemingly unendingly, with a marvellous rising boom from the exhaust, and the dead back axle and chain final drive puts more power down without any problems of torque reaction and not a trace of wheelspin even on tight corners. It is apparently totally manageable, and quite magnificent. I can only echo Kent Karlslake's remark, after driving Black Bess [one of the subsequent production of five-liter cars], that it is a tragedy that Bugatti abandoned the big four-cylinder car."

I purchased the dismantled parts of my car from collector Peter Hampton in 1974. Close study of the photographs taken in 1912, some of which show every detail, proved that these were indeed the parts of this same car. Surprisingly little had been lost during its years in pieces. Even the radiator was still there, undamaged and still bearing a plate with the words "Automobil Kühler—Patent—Dr. Zimmerman—Ludwigshaven-am-Rhein." The body was missing but a new one was made which is an exact copy of the 1912 version.

The four-cylinder engine of 100 by 160 mm (5026 cc) has a five-bearing crankshaft, an overhead cam mounted in five ball races and driven from the front by a vertical shaft and bevel gears. There are two inlet valves and one exhaust valve per cylinder, the valves operated by rocker cam fingers. Totally enclosed, the whole design is remarkably advanced for its date and has more in common with the famous Grand Prix Bugattis of the Twenties than with the contemporary Type 13 production car engine. The one major failing was the lubrication system.

A large worm-driven piston pump was mounted on the back of the firewall driven from the camshaft, and this pump did a good job of lubricating the camshaft through twelve jets, one aimed at each cam lobe. Lubrication of the crankshaft, however, was almost overlooked. A metered quantity of oil was introduced into the crankcase on the outside of the cylinder barrel extensions, and then fell into the sump. Since the crankcase and sump assembly is circular in cross-section, following the path of the crankcase webs, the oil was thrown

about by the connecting rods and was then supposed to find its way into little trays, one on the top of each big-end, machined from the solid rod billet, and one above each main journal.

With no sump reservoir, any excess oil was either thrown out of the breathers or found its way into a large box on the nearside where it could seek refuge until the engine stopped. When I came to restore the car, I found it was possible to give the engine a pressure-fed dry sump system without damaging or modifying any original part, and I have done this without apology, so that I can now drive the car without fear of imminent disaster.

The transmission is from a multi-plate clutch of typical Bugatti design which he had perfected for Deutz, using cruciform joints to a very beautiful gearbox. Bugatti's earlier gearbox design for the chain-driven Deutz was mechanically similar to the gearbox he made for his own car, but Bugatti was an artist first and an engineer afterwards. He took great trouble to make this gearbox a thing of beauty. No other Bugatti, perhaps no other car, has had a gearbox whose shape is so close to pure sculpture, yet so completely practical, containing as it does not only the gears (parallel input and output shafts with no layshaft) but also the crown wheel, pinion and differential with another pinion behind the crown wheel to drive the transmission brake.

The final drive by chain is virtually identical to Bugatti's similar designs for Deutz, except that the Deutz semi-elliptic springs were replaced by re-

versed quarter-elliptic springs, a classic Bugatti feature, though it was not used for the production cars until late in 1913. The rear axle, curiously, is designed to give the rear wheels slight camber.

Steering is through a well-designed steering box with ball bearings taking all radial and thrust loads, and the front axle supports the car on two slender springs each side, attached at the front to delicate dumb irons of typical Bugatti elegance, in contrast to the Deutz front end used on the 1910 Prince Henry car.

At some time in 1912, Bugatti's close friend Roland Garros, a very famous aviator renowned throughout France, saw the car and asked Bugatti to make him another like it. Bugatti designed a two-seat touring car with a longer chassis and a number of modifications to the engine, and by mid-1913 he had completed this second car. As it was for sale, it was entered in the factory records with the number 474 (the first production Type 13 had the number 361, so this was the 113th number allocated). The fact that Bugatti's own original car is entered in the factory records as 471, and stamped with this number, although the car had already been in use for three years, is most easily explained by the likelihood that Bugatti did not bother to number his own personal racing car until it was clear that he was going to make another of the same type.

The major difference between the Garros car and the earlier one was in the lubrication system, which was even then seen to be unsatisfactory. Garros' 474 had a full rectangular oil reservoir in the sump and jet lubrication of the bearings, but only three main bearings. Three more cars similar to 474 were made during 1914, with the numbers 714, 715 and 716. The history of the original car, 471, after its heyday in 1912, is that it stayed at Molsheim until the outbreak of war in 1914, when Bugatti sold it to the Duke of Bavaria, who removed the curious pointed-tail racing body and had a more comfortable touring body made which appears to have been the work of Durr of Colmar. During the Twenties it was bought by Bruno Martinelli of Chiasso, a Swiss border town north of Milan. Martinelli was a champion racing motorcyclist who was killed in a race at Geneva in 1936, which was when the car was bought by Colonel Giles and brought in pieces to England. Colonel

Giles already owned the Garros car, known by then as Black Bess, and both cars eventually came into the hands of Peter Hampton, from whom I bought 471.

Of the other four cars, two survive. The Garros car—474—which came to England in the Twenties, was raced at Brooklands by Miss Ivy Cummings and was named Black Bess by her. Number 715 remained at Molsheim in chassis form until 1963 when it was bought by Schlumph and is now in the Schlumph museum at Mulhouse in France. Numbers 714 and 716 were both raced at Indianapolis, 714 in 1914 and 716 in 1915. The 1914 car, driven by Bugatti's longtime associate

Ernst Friedrich, had its engine bored out to yield a 390-cubic-inch capacity. The car started in eighteenth position but was in third place after 425 miles when, according to Friedrich, "the ball bearings on the driving pinion" broke. The car is believed to have returned to Molsheim. Chassis 716 raced with its engine displacing the normal five liters or 300 cubic inches. Driven by George Hill, it failed after twenty-two laps when the water pump broke. The car later raced on the West Coast. It may even now be in some barn awaiting discovery. If it is found, we will be able to add another piece to the story of these unusually fast and fascinating Edwardian automobiles.⚜

scale 1/43

a survey for collectors by david sinclair

If you have even a passing interest in automotive miniatures, chances are you're aware that this hobby has expanded and matured in recent years. The addition of new offerings, the delightfully cosmopolitan flavor of the pastime, the ever escalating prices for rarer models, the increasing popularity of flea markets devoted only to model cars; all have tended to create a kind of boom in collecting. Yet despite its increasing popularity, the hobby itself is not a new one.

For almost as long as automobiles have been manufactured, there have been toy or model cars built as well. As far back as 1878, the Bing Company in Germany produced tin-plate cars with spring motors, steering, brakes and leaf springs that worked. These and many other priceless antique toy cars are very rare today and can be found only in museums or private collections.

More readily available to the new collector are die cast metal cars produced since the Thirties. While these pre-assembled models are, and have been, made in many scales, the most popular size worldwide has been 1/43, averaging from 3½- to 4½-inches overall. Models of this general size were first produced in the United States during the Twenties and Thirties by Tootsietoy. While these little objects were more toys than scale models, they at least were usually recognizable as miniatures of the cars whose names they bore. Toy cars by other manufacturers of the era hold little interest for the average collector since they rarely resembled any real car but looked instead like something out of a science fiction movie, designed as they were to appeal only to the imagination of youngsters.

It has been only during the past twenty years that any firms have produced miniature cars with the collector market foremost in mind. Even today, most of the large firms are primarily interested in the large "toy" market rather than the market for scale models. But an increasing number of adults now collect such "toys" as they become ever more authentic looking.

Chief among firms making models such as these are Dinky Toys of England—begun in 1933—Corgi, and Lesney which began operation in the Fifties. All three have enjoyed good distribution throughout the world and Lesney's "Matchbox" trademark has almost become a generic term. Until the early Sixties, these imports from England were virtually the only miniature cars to be found in America. While they were considerably more sophisticated than anything that had been made in this country, they were still basically toys.

None of these firms maintained constant scale within their lines, ranging around 1/43 but often made to fit a standard size box with the result that a Volkswagen could become the same size as a Rolls-Royce. Their colors also left much to be desired from a collector's standpoint, for the manufacturers seemed to feel that the brighter they were, the better the models would sell. Thus it was not unusual to see metallic lavender Mercers, candy apple red Bentleys and other unlikely paint jobs. Interiors tended to be baby blue or pink rather than realistic black or tan. Despite this, some adults began collecting them in the United States.

In Europe, however, collectors had been enjoying more realistic miniature cars for many years. As early as 1920, the French firm, CD, was making lead 1/43 scale cars and Citroën made miniatures of their big cars, producing some forty-four dif-

photography by stan grayson with art direction by theodore r.f. hall

Veterans in plastic: At the left is an 1897 Tatra by Igra of Czechoslovakia. At the right is an 1894 Benz Omnibus by Cursor of Germany.

Rio's 1894 De Dion-Bouton. From Safir of France, a '10 Grégoire. Lesney's '12 Ford and '18 Crossley.

ferent models in lead, plaster and flour, and pressed steel during the years 1926-1935. André Citroën's philosophy was that if a French child had a toy Citroën to play with, he might buy a real one when he grew up. There were other model makers as well.

I began learning about the many lines of automotive miniatures manufactured in Europe during the early Sixties, and at that time decided to leave my job to establish a mail order business specializing in these often hard-to-get models from Italy, France, West Germany, Denmark, Spain

and other countries. Rio, the first company I contacted, then had a line of about seventeen models, most of them Fiats, Alfa Romeos, Isottas, Italas and other cars of ancient vintage. At that time, only R. Gordon & Co., a book store in New York, had ever imported Rio models and the cars were basically known only to Gordon's customers.

Rio was at first hesitant about selling to a mail order firm, pleading that its production was too limited to satisfy the huge American market. The people there suggested that it would be better to

wait a couple of years until they were able to increase production before ads began to appear in American publications. When they were assured that only a small start was envisioned and that the Rio name would be gradually introduced to the American collector, they began making shipments. The models were an immediate sensation. Never before had such quality and realism been seen. Today, the Rio line numbers sixty-nine antique and classic cars. When a 1941 Lincoln Continental convertible and a Duesenberg SJ dual cowl phaeton

Two from Brumm. Ford's 999 and Cugnot's artillery tractor of 1769. The 1898 Fiat was made by Dugu.

were added, these models became Rio's fastest sellers in America.

Following Rio's successful introduction, the products of other European companies were made available. Dugu, also of Italy, built a small line of vintage cars during the Sixties. While not quite of Rio's quality, these were interesting models, for example, a 1912 Itala touring car with a brass serpent's head horn so popular with sports of that day. Dugu also produced a beautiful Lancia Lambda and after much discussion with me, a Duesenberg

town car and Cord 812. There were other Italian firms too: Edil, EGM, Icis, SAM-TOY, all of which are apparently out of business today. Very few of these models ever found their way to America.

Models by Polistil, however, did. This company, a very large Italian toy manufacturer and one of the most prolific of die cast firms, produced about 100 different plastic models in a rather odd 1/41 scale during 1960-1964. From 1965 through 1969, about 100 metal models in 1/43 were made, many

of them duplicating those previously offered in plastic. This was the Polistil "M" series, among the finest contemporary models ever. Many featured wire spoke wheels; all were painted in realistic colors. Doors, hoods and trunks opened and fidelity was as near perfect as could be found in small scale.

Polistil, however, produces most of its items for only a couple of years and then stops to devote assembly lines to something new. Today the emphasis is on 1/25 scale and larger, with very few

The rare Hanomag was an offering by Ziss of Germany. The Morgan and Eldridge's '23 Fiat are by Brumm. The 1914 Panhard-Levassor is one of Minialuxe's all-plastic offerings.

1/43 models being made. One of the most outstanding Politoy "M" models was number 532, an Alfa Romeo Grand Sport Zagato. The doors opened, the hood was center-hinged and revealed a detailed engine and the steering worked. This rare model is among those illustrated here.

Two other Italian firms which make contemporary cars are Mercury and Mebetoy; the latter has produced some fine models with beautiful paint finishes including the Corvette Rondine Pininfarina. When Mattel bought Mebetoy, the American toy firm ordered that the models be made to sell at a price which would bring mass volume over-the-counter sales in America. Mebetoys today bear little resemblance to those of the Sixties, except for their basic shapes. The fine detail and finish is gone; the wheels no longer have the realistic appearance they once did and, in general, the models are not of the calibre realized when Mebetoy was independent.

In 1975, the supply of Rio models began to seriously dwindle. Part of the cause was the horrendous labor problem in Italy. But much of it could be blamed on the apathetic outlook of Rio's owners; the Tattarletti family apparently viewed the models as a sideline to keep its workers busy when other business interests slowed. Then Reno Tat-

tarletti left the family business to start his own firm, Brumm.

He initially offered two series, an "Old Fire" line of ancient steam-powered vehicles like the Cugnot wagon, and the "Revival" series of automobiles like the Morgan three-wheeler and Bédélia cyclecar. Now a third line, "Revival Gold" has been added featuring historic racing cars such as Locomobile "Old 16," various Grand Prix Fiats

and Oldfield's 1909 Blitzen Benz. Brumm also makes a magnificent line of 1/43 scale horse-drawn carriages. Apparently all these new releases in a comparatively short time put a little fire under Rio; recently that company's models have become a bit easier to obtain. And finally some new models were released, too, including the Ford "999" racer. Brumm happened to release its own version of that historic car at the same time and legal battles began

between the two sides of the Tattarletti family. It is rumored that Rio has won and that Brumm's version will not be available when present inventories are exhausted in the United States. If that is true, Brumm's Ford "999" will become a valuable piece very quickly.

France is another large producer of 1/43 scale cars, although many manufacturers there have also gone out of business over the years. Today the prin-

cipal French manufacturer is Solido. In addition to a line of twenty-three classic cars, that company also offers a sizeable assortment of contemporary and racing cars. Its classics, while not quite as highly detailed as Rio's, are sturdier, lacking the many tiny parts which grace the Italian firm's products. Unfortunately the current Solido distributor in the United States is importing only a few of the line's contemporary cars this year. These lovely models are noteworthy for, among other things, the fact that each has appropriate wheels; some manufacturers make do with one or two wheel designs for every model.

For many years, the Solido company was managed by the very attractive and charming Madame Wahl whom I had the pleasure of meeting at the Paris Toy Fair. Apparently a Paris bank has now taken control of Solido and Madame Wahl has resigned. This is not unusual, a rather high proportion of model-making firms have experienced severe financial problems or have gone bankrupt.

One of the reasons for this is the rather high initial investment required, an investment which must be recouped by successful distribution and sales. Dies for a single model cost from $40,000 to $50,000 today. It is also necessary to invest in very expensive automated equipment for casting, finishing and painting. If a firm suffers labor problems, poor management or distribution, or is not able to turn over its inventory fast enough to have capital for reinvestment in dies for new models, staying in business becomes difficult.

The most recent French entry into 1/43 is Jacques Greilsamer's Eligor Models consisting of some sixteen quite interesting subjects including a Peugeot 201, Hotchkiss and the Citroën Rosalie pictured here. While not quite up to Rio or Solido standards, the fidelity of these Eligor models is excellent and the company plans to issue some never-before-seen cars including a 1937 Panhard Dynamic sedan and Delage D 8 SS roadster.

Norev of France produces models of contemporary cars in both metal and plastic although the latter have seldom been imported to the United States since they duplicate the metal versions. At this time, there is no Norev importer here. During the Sixties the company offered plastic models of various cars from the Twenties and Thirties but production of this delightful line has been discontinued, to the regret of collectors everywhere.

A line of plastic French models of vintage cars still available is Minialuxe whose products are comparatively inexpensive. Plastic is a suitable material for models of really old cars since metal can be a bit too thick for some spidery parts. R.A.M.I., however, produced an enchanting series of all-metal antique cars, a grouping of which accompanies our story. This firm too has been out of business for some time. Safir, which also offered beautiful models of older cars made of composite metal and plastic, is heard from only rarely and the models are seldom available in America. A little French company whose models are available in the United States is Dubray, which markets a limited number of "Airflow" Peugeots that are made by hand.

The largest Scandinavian model maker was the Danish firm of Tekno which offered over 400 models from 1949 until its demise in 1972. Although some of the cars differed only in their decal decoration, the quality of all was high and Tekno probably offered the best 1/43 Jaguar XK-E, not to mention a fine Mustang. Toronado and Volvo P1800. After bankruptcy, a few of the company's truck and bus model dies found their way to the Netherlands. The models were available for a brief time but delivery was so sporadic that the American distributor became discouraged and gave up. One of the more unique Tekno trucks was a Ford D-800 tilt-cab decorated for Tuborg Beer. It featured thirty-two removable beer cases.

Germany, naturally, has contributed a number of die cast manufacturers, although at present activity there is in decline. The old firm of Schuco, famous for its ingenious tin plate mechanical cars, began offering a 1/43 die cast line a few years ago. These were high quality models but production costs and mismanagement soon forced Schuco into bankruptcy. The models, mostly German cars like Audis, Rabbits and BMW's, escalated in price as soon as the bankruptcy was announced. The firm's Porsche 924 is one of the most difficult of recently produced models to find.

A grouping of all-metal horseless carriage models by R.A.M.I. of France. From left to right: 1898 Hautier electric, 1900 De Dion-Bouton, 1895 Panhard-Levassor, 1899 Gobron-Brillie, 1906 Sizaire-Naudin, 1898 Gauthier-Wehrle, 1895 Rochet-Schneider.

Märklin, the company famous for its HO and Z gauge electric trains, also made a line of die cast 1/43 automobiles for a few years but rather quickly discontinued it to concentrate on the railroad business. The models, mostly of German sedans, were excellent but used only a couple of wheel patterns which detracted somewhat from their desirability.

Ziss, a comparatively small family operation, made a line of 1/43 antique cars plus a few modern vehicles. Noteworthy were a boattail Audi Alpensieger and a tiny 1924 Hanomag which is shown here. Like so many other companies, Ziss apparently fell on hard times and nothing has been heard from this German firm for the past few years.

One of the few West German firms still active is

Gama. The fidelity of its models varies but a wide range is offered in various scales with only a limited number available in the United States.

In Spain, Solido models were made under license by Dalia but the line was never seen to any extent in this country. Auto-Pilen does make an excellent line of models with fine paint finishes and more opening features than generally offered these days. The company's 1963 Corvette coupé is especially popular in America.

Even Russia's Diwi is producing a line of 1/43 die cast cars and they have been available in the United States for a number of years. They are all variations of the Moskvich or the Lada and rather well done too. U.S. Customs charges almost four times the duty on these models as on die casts from

other countries. It is a heady seventy percent, rather incongruous since the duty on the real cars, which may be imported next year, will be only ten percent.

In Britain, Lesney produces the most reasonably-priced line of metal vintage car models in the world. This year they released a new series painted, at last, in authentic colors. The purist will now be able to place a Matchbox model alongside a Rio or Solido without making apologies for it. Sure to be popular in the United States are an all-new Cord 812, an Auburn and a Stutz. A Model T delivery van with Coca Cola livery will also be available.

Corgi developed a small line of excellent antique cars in Britain during 1963-1964. The series included a 1927 Bentley Three-Litre Le Mans in two versions, a 1915 Ford Model T in three colors—black included and the most sought after today—a 1910 Daimler, 1910 Renault and an exquisite 1912 Rolls-Royce. Unfortunately a fire destroyed all the dies for these models and Corgi never made new ones. Consequently the models have been off the market for years.

Dinky, the English pioneer of the industry, produced models of approximately 1/43 scale, but today seems concerned only with somewhat larger sizes. The company's vast offerings of the past, both pre- and post-war, have become immensely popular collectables of great value. There is material enough in this subject to warrant an entire book, and at least one has, in fact, been published. Dinky Toys have also been produced in France.

All the models mentioned thus far have been made by commercial firms using "mass production" methods. While their combined output has been in the thousands of different models and in the hundreds of various marques, these still represent only a fraction of the number of real cars produced since the beginning of the automotive age. Again, the investment in tooling costs has been a factor.

To produce a model die cast car, engineers and designers make initial studies requiring several months, sometimes up to two years. The prototype is carved from wood, usually slightly larger than the ultimate casting will be. The wooden model then is utilized to make a resin casting which is baked and used to produce a matrix. Then toolmakers, with pantographs, reduce this casting to the desired scale. A jeweler's eye-piece and

Page opposite, the rare and wonderful Alfa Romeo 1750 once offered by Politoys of Italy. It has steerable front wheels, opening doors and hood, highly-detailed undercarriage. Above, Lesney's 1906 Rolls-Royce Silver Ghost and a 1912 Rolls-Royce town car. Below is a rakish 1932 Bugatti Type 50 successfully modelled by Italy's Rio.

Here are two of the classic car models offered by Solido of France. Above is one of the most recent, a Mercedes-Benz 540K. Below is the distinctive Voisin 17CV of 1934. Both are primarily made of metal, like all this firm's models. Although still available, products by Solido have undergone a price increase due to a management change.

measuring apparatus accurate to one micron, and an exceedingly fine drill bit, assure a faithful reproduction of the original model.

The mold, made of vanadium/chrome steel must be able to withstand the action of cold water, molten metal and hot air under pressure simultaneously. The mold is placed on an automatic injection press; some molds can produce up to 10,000 units per day. The metal used is known as Zamac, an alloy of zinc plus four percent aluminum, one percent copper and .03 percent magnesium. It is introduced in ingots into the crucible, brought to melting and injected under pressure into the mold.

The rough cast parts are then automatically ejected from the presses and sent to the trimming and polishing departments. From there, they go on to the paint shops which also use automated machines. Then the models are dried. Even bumpers, headlights, taillights and radiators are painted by machines using a semi-automatic electronic system. All this equipment costs hundreds of thousands or even millions of dollars. Thus, once more, it can be seen why your own particular favorite car may not have been offered as a model. Cost.

A few years ago, a number of European collectors skilled at scratch building decided to try and offer some models not available from the bigger companies. Not having the capital to invest in costly dies, they built originals in brass and from these made vulcanized rubber molds. Utilizing an alloy called white metal which contains some lead, they filled the mold and used centrifugal force to drive out bubbles and voids. The rubber molds can withstand only 700 degrees Fahrenheit, not the 900 degrees at which Zamac is injected, and they are good for some 400 to 1000 castings before they must be replaced. Unless the small entrepreneur has the talent and skill to make the master in brass, the cost for having this done is about $1000. The rubber molds are inexpensive, however, only some seven dollars, with raw materials for each model about three dollars. All finishing of pieces is done by hand and assembled models usually cost several times the price of a kit or mass-produced model. Even the kits are comparatively expensive.

These models, usually produced in someone's kitchen or basement, have been referred to by the Italian collectors' club magazine *Quattroroutine* as *"modelli speciali."* It is not easy to estimate how many people making them are active at a given

*Opposite, a 1933 Citroën Rosalie modelled by Eligor of France.
Above, a Saab from Denmark's Tekno, once among the most prolific
of manufacturers but long since out of business today. Below, a
Land Rover with special decoration, once available from Politoys.*

*Like most Corgi models, the Mini Cooper above is rather larger
than 1/43rd. It and many other offerings by this British firm
are no longer available. The Moskvitch 427, below, is one of
several models of Russian automobiles currently being imported.*

A classic trio: Lesney's 1930 Duesenberg, Brooklin's 1932 Packard, and Rio's 1934 Duesenberg. Opposite: Brooklin's latest, a 1940 Chrysler Newport show car, Lesney's new 815 Auburn and 812 Cord, a charming 1909 Chalmers-Detroit by Rio and a 1930 Ford Model A by Brooklin, one of this Canadian maker's growing model lineup.

time since they tend to come and go rather quickly but there are probably two or three dozen in Italy, France, England, Germany, Canada and the United States. Most of these models are available only as kits which, while apparently popular in Europe, have not met with much success in America where few collectors seem interested in construction which requires laborious assembly, filing and painting.

Two firms making these models seem to have graduated from the kitchen or basement category to become small business enterprises with a reasonable number of employees and dependable delivery. Western Models Ltd. of England which began about 1973 now offers over three dozen different models with prices starting at thirty-five dollars and a delivery time usually of about eight weeks. Their quality has consistently improved over the past six years and the models now feature "glass" windows, unlike the earliest examples. Still, they do not have all the delectable minutiae of a Rio model.

In Canada, a young man named John Hall started Brooklin Models a few years ago. He planned to concentrate on American classic and special interest cars, believing quite rightly that there was no shortage of European cars available and that American collectors would be a good market. His early models lacked "glass" windows but he too has steadily improved his product and the quality

today is high. The line is still small, only eight models at this time but each one is interesting and unique. One of them is featured on the cover of this issue.

Activity in the "special model" area in the United States has been severely limited. A firm known as Nostalgic Miniatures has produced a few 1/43 items, but mostly its offerings have been in 1/50 and the models have not always been painted but made instead of pewter. Another firm, Marque Products, has produced a few white metal kits in 1/43. While not a manufacturer of "special models," a craftsman in the United States named Bob MacLeay offers a line of modified Rio and Solido models which he painstakingly converts to different body styles and superdetails. These are expensive, costing fifty dollars and up, depending on the time he must devote to a given conversion.

How many people are collecting miniatures today? There are probably at least 50,000 in the United States alone who have a few models at least. The hobby is now very popular in Europe and Japan. Collectors have found their models to be excellent investments with some of them appreciating at a faster rate—in terms of percentages—than the real thing. A Swiss collector recently sold a collection of 3000 die cast cars for $60,000, an average of twenty dollars per model although he no doubt bought many of them for a dollar or two some years ago. The Tootsietoy LaSalle and Grahams

Above: the AC Aceca coupé was made by Dinky of England, the pioneer die-casting firm. At left is a Ferrari Boxer Berlinetta by Solido. Below is the BMW 2000CS once offered by the Belgian firm of Sablon and the '63 Corvette by Pilen of Spain. Page opposite: Ferrari 512M by Solido.

which sold for ten cents in the Thirties regularly command as much as seventy-five dollars today. Demand being what it is, there are even some replicas of the originals being produced at more modest prices.

Generally speaking, values begin to rise as soon as the model is taken out of production. The Dugu Cord, for instance, was a sensation at six dollars in the early Seventies. Now that Dugu is out of business, that model commands some sixty dollars. Rarely has anyone attempted to publish a price guide to die cast cars in general. The few existing ones deal with a single manufacturer's products such as Dinky or Lesney and, in some cases, the quoted values are open to serious question. Like the real thing, miniature car values really depend on how much a given buyer is willing to pay. Neither is there a comprehensive list of every model ever offered. Three dedicated Porsche model collectors compiled a list of some 1600 models in all scales but not since 1967 has anyone tried to publish a complete list of every model ever made.

For those who seek "obsolete" models, the swap meets being held around the country for dealers

and collectors are favorite haunts. Often those who have particularly rare items prefer to swap for a rare model they desire than try to establish dollar values. There are also swap sheets filled with "wanted" and "for sale" ads plus the lists of items mailed out occasionally by collectors who do a certain amount of buying and selling. Since stores specializing in these models are so rare, especially in the United States, mail order is the most common way of obtaining models, whether new or old.

As of 1979, the hobby has grown increasingly sophisticated and expensive. Whether it remains a true hobby or becomes an avocation for the wealthy and the speculator, like the old car hobby in general, remains to be seen. But the charm of these models for many in all walks of life remains undeniable. Built by companies all over the world, they enable one to concentrate on virtually any area of automotive interest, whether a single marque or a collection tracing the history of the self-propelled vehicle from its earliest days to the present. The hobby has, in fact, coalesced into a worldwide group of enthusiasts who, whatever their background or language, share a common passion. ✤

Sammy

Say Sammy Davis to anyone today, even a motorist, and his mind will immediately fly to the upper echelons of the international entertainment industry and one of its most successful luminaries. But to have said the same name thirty or forty years ago or, come to that, fifty or sixty years ago, to anyone who held a steering wheel with something less than distaste—and a quite different figure sprang to mind.

That great gentleman who so dominated European motoring in the years between the wars was, at one and the same time, an engineer and a mechanic, an artist and a cartoonist, a journalist and an author, a racing driver and a team manager—and so much else besides, that imagination boggles at the extent of his capacity. Of all the things he did, he will probably be best remembered as a driver at Le Mans and other long-distance sports car races, and he was certainly one of the best that ever lived.

One must be careful not to say "greatest," for that is a word which Sammy does not much hold with in this connection. He has had all his life, and still has, a very singular view of the racing driver and his place in the scheme of things. Of all the men in the game, he is the most prone in his old age to say that things today are splendid. He does not look back and try to convince you that things were much better in the past. But for all that, he insisted then—and insists now—that it is the car that wins the race and not the driver. Strange as this may seem in a world of Andrettis and Hunts, it was a commonly held view in the great days of Le Mans, and you only have to glance at a newspaper of the time to know that Bentley won again, with no mention until after the third paragraph of who the drivers might have been—even if one of them was Sammy Davis.

Sidney Charles Houghton Davis was born in London on the 9th of January 1887, though in fact his family came from Hull, on the northeast coast of England, and it was there that he spent much of his early youth. The Davises, as one might expect from this particular member of the family, were a fairly bright lot and Sammy's grandparents owned and ran a sizeable department store in the town of Hull. Their life appears to have been happy and the children well content, though there are some curious tales which make good reading. It appears that Grandpa was away from home a good deal one way or another and, on his return to the family fold, his luggage was usually unpacked by a faithful manservant. However, on one occasion, this gentleman was not available and Sammy's grandmother did the job, only to discover, mixed up in her husband's clothing, what are described as a singularly naughty pair of ladies knickers. Grandma went off thereafter to the family store to make some purchases, which she often did, signing the bill in the process. This time, however, she went to the dress department and bought herself some outrageously attractive and outstandingly expensive garments. Returning home, she placed the bill on her husband's desk as usual but attached to it, with a pin,

the offending undergarments. Nothing is ever supposed to have been said about this event, but something must have been—or Sammy would never have got hold of the story.

The children had a pretty free run of the house and when they got into trouble for their wilder pranks, they had their own way of dealing with it. It would appear that Sammy's sister, who had large blue eyes, was especially good at explaining away their misdemeanors and once when they decided to toboggan down the main stairway on a tray and did considerable damage to the walls and bannisters, it was sister who was sent to "explain" what had happened. Nevertheless, for all she did for the boys, Sammy did not always please her. Apart from anything else, he had a long-standing desire to drive a fire engine and, believing that if he were to succeed in that profession he had better get some practice first, he set fire to his sister's doll house and then came in on some toy engine or other to put it out. This was not well received.

Nor was the occasion when he and his brother decided to raid their money boxes by the cunning device of spreading butter on a knife and turning the box upside down and getting out such coin as stuck to the knife when they withdrew it. This would have been all right had the money box not been a joint one for all the children. Sammy's sister was outraged to find that *her* money was being pillaged. She was not at all mollified by Sammy's suggestion that she had not thought of the idea, and the person who did was entitled to the loot.

Despite fond memories of the family home in the north, Sammy's parents lived in London and it was from there that he went to Westminster School under the shadow of Westminster Abbey before being confronted with thinking up something to do for a livelihood. Sammy's mother was the daughter of a well-known painter; he himself had been taught to draw and paint by her and found it came very naturally to him. It was not surprising that he decided, if possible, he would like to make art his career; to this end he was sent to the Slade School, one of the most famous art schools in London then as now. Among the first things Sammy learned, however, was that there was no money to be made out of painting until you were famous; he quickly came to the conclusion that starvation was likely to come before fame and that he had better therefore think of something else.

As he had also developed an interest in motorcars and motorcycles, this seemed a likely direction in which to turn. His motorcycling had in fact taken place in North London together with a young friend by the name of W.O. Bentley. Together they had raced their motorcycles round the northern suburbs to the fury of the population. This included W.O. Bentley's father who on one occasion, maddened by the noise, hurled the family Bible out of the window narrowly missing the boys, after which Sammy was banned from the house for some time and W.O. had to go and stay with cousins.

Having decided that the motorcar was to be his future, Sammy asked his father if something could not be done to get him an apprenticeship in a motor

by Michael Frostick

works. By good fortune his father knew the head of the Daimler company and Sammy was duly sent to see this august gentleman for an interview. Unfortunately, he decided to go on his motorcycle which was not working very well, so he arrived covered in oil and in some trepidation. However this turned out to be all for the best since when Sir Edward Manville, the gentleman in question, saw him, he simply said, "well, since you're covered with oil already and obviously full of enthusiasm we'll take you on as an apprentice"—and nothing could have suited Sammy better.

He found the people with whom he was to work at Daimler very much to his liking, being straightforward and honest men, although he claims they had never met anybody before who had three Christian names. Casting away the two they found difficult to pronounce, they settled quite happily for the fact that he was to be Charlie, and Charlie he might well have remained had he not been sent upstairs to the purchasing office soon thereafter to get something that was required for an experimental model. There was a lady secretary up there of a rather forbidding aspect, who took one look at his filthy overalls and said, "you're not coming in here, little black Sambo, you stay outside." And it was from this that he eventually became Sambo, and that in turn changed to Sammy by which name he has been known ever since—although in fact it is not his name at all.

It was while he was in apprenticeship at Daimler that he met another man who was to be a colleague all his life and who was to have a great influence on what he did. That person was the famous artist Gordon Crosby. Crosby was not taking to life at Daimler quite as well as Sammy and eventually announced that he was going off to get a job with a magazine. This horrified Sammy and he said so. The very idea that anyone who was destined for such a high calling as engineering could lower himself to associate in any way with the press seemed absolutely dreadful, at least until Sammy discovered how much Crosby was going to be paid. The magnificent sum of something like £5 a week seemed a king's ransom, and Sammy decided that the only sensible thing was

to throw caution to the winds and join his friend, so he went off himself to part of the same organization to become an illustrator.

The magazine which Sammy Davis joined was *The Automobile Engineer* which had only just then come onto the bookstalls. Here he found himself also working with Gordon Crosby because, although Crosby was on *The Autocar*, in those days it didn't matter so much what paper you were on; they were all owned by Iliffe and in the same building, so there was a good deal of flexibility. Things might well have stopped there had not the editor, a man by the name of Claydon, suddenly come to Sammy one day and said, "well, now you're going to write." Sammy was up in arms immediately: "I can't do that," he said, "I've had a public school education, I can't even spell." "Never mind, said Claydon, "you're going to write. You will go away and you will do a description of the new Fafnir and you've got two weeks to do it in."

At this point Sammy was a bit downcast but then, as he now describes it, he had the idea of the century. He simply got hold of another paper which had already done a description of the car and although he is adamant that he didn't copy it exactly, he would be the first to admit that he followed it very closely. To his considerable surprise, this went down very well with the editor, so that from that moment onwards Sammy was a writer as well as an illustrator and exactly where he would have proceeded from there, we can't tell. Because the First World War then intervened.

Like all other young men of his age, Sammy went off to fight for King and Country and, like so many other young men, suffered badly in the process. It was not very long before he was back in England badly wounded, and suffering from poison gas. After a longish period in hospital, he was regarded as more or less fit and a job had to be found for him. This came from whomever was responsible for supervision of aeroplane engine production and on the basis that he knew a lot about internal combustion engines, the first thing he was told to do was "go down to Gwynne's and see what that officer Bentley is doing—and by the way we'll make you responsible to see that they're building the engines properly."

This of course was a piece of pure good fortune; Sammy was more than happy to help his friend with this vital effort. He was no doubt partially responsible for getting W.O. Bentley moved from Gwynne's to Humber's where the famous BR1 and BR2 engines were eventually built, but the strain of the work was too much for Sammy's scarcely repaired health and it was not long before he was back in hospital again. None of this, however, had damped his enthusiasm for either the motorcar or for fast motoring and, when the war was over, he returned to *The Autocar* to become its first sports editor and since at that time the magazine published no one's name, he was required to produce a pseudonym for himself. He could think of nothing much but as he had recently had a crash helmet in his hand, he chose to call himself "Casque" by which name he was known until he left the magazine after the Second World War.

Surprisingly, when it came to racing, the magazine was not against his participation, which was the exact opposite of *The Motor* which belonged to a different firm, Temple Press, where Rodney Walkerly was quite forbidden to participate in anything. In Sammy's case, the magazine was happy as long as he did not drive continuously for one firm, and this he certainly avoided. *The Autocar* was also anxious that he should not drive for foreign manufacturers and as this idea was in accordance with Sammy's own, there were no conflicts, and he embarked upon a racing career of almost unparalleled virtuosity.

He drove so many cars in so many races for so many different people that to try and catalogue the results would require a huge volume and become tedious rather than exciting, but nevertheless the highlights are worth a reminder. He started as a good racing driver should, in those far-off days, by taking records, mostly at Brooklands circuit and the first one with an AC. He went as a riding mechanic with Count Zborowski in a Miller at the French Grand Prix in 1924 and then by some quirk of fate Louis Coatalen let him have a go round the outer circuit of Brooklands in one of the big twelve-cylinder Sunbeams, a car which Sammy says "was sheer animal which simply tried to assassinate you if you had not previously coaxed it into the right temper and then handled it carefully. Yet in its day it was one of the most wonderful cars in the world which gave you, as nothing else could, a sense of terrific power, hurling one round the track at real speed. It went down the railway straight at 140 mph so that the car taught me that, provided one went fast enough, Brooklands track needed as much knowing as the road. Indeed Coatalen's instructions were 'drive as if you were on the road.'"

As a result of this escapade, Coatalen offered Sammy a drive on the Sunbeam team for the 1925 Le Mans 24 Hours, in which he and his co-driver Chassagne managed to finish second, beating the Bentleys. This led to W.O. giving him a drive on the Bentley team the following year when, to his utter chagrin, he crashed the car. He got it stuck in the sand and no one could get it out. In his own words, "it was hopeless, nobody could budge the car at the time singlehanded. Feeling thoroughly ill, I had to go to the pits in the official car where I felt worse because the Lorraine team and the crowd cheered. I met W.O.'s eyes and felt worse still. I said, 'I have made a fool of myself and broken up the car' and then I went for a long walk alone and wished I was dead."

But for all that, W.O. evidently forgave him for he was back on the same team in 1927, the year of the memorable White House crash and the legendary victory at Le Mans. And so the list goes on. He was second in a Lea Francis in the Dublin races in 1929, he was second in a Bentley in the 500-mile race at Brooklands the same year, and he won the same race there in 1930 driving a supercharged Austin Seven. He was second in a Talbot the year following with Brian Lewis; and, also driving a Bentley, he was second in the Double Twelve at Brooklands both in 1929 and 1930, the first time with Sir Ronald Gunter and the second time with Clive Dunfee. He had an appalling crash in a short race at Brooklands in 1931, which put him into hospital for some time, and perhaps led to his doing more work as a team manager after that. But he continued to drive in reliability trials. He drove in the Monte Carlo Rally; he was one of the founders of the London-Brighton run and indeed went on driving his famous tricycle Beelzebub until many years after the Second World War when he was already attaining a great age.

Bright as he is for a man over ninety, memory is beginning to fade. But some of those tremendous moments remain as clear with him today as ever they were and what he has to say about them now, in the light of experience, is more than ever fascinating. Going back to his first crash in the Bentley he says, "and then W.O. asked me to drive one of his cars, because with the Sunbeam I had succeeded in beating his cars in the first race. The trouble was that the brakes failed, they failed utterly; and I was a damn fool really. I got a signal saying we could be third if I could go faster, so I tried to overtake the Lorraine and did, but I shouldn't have done. When I found I wasn't going to get round the corner I should have gone down the escape road and had another shot; but I didn't, I tried to make the corner and got the car stuck in the sand; and you know I couldn't dig it out again."

And thus you are back to the sorrows that he wrote about many years before. One might well imagine that, asked for the highlight of his career, Sammy would turn to Le Mans in 1927 and the White House crash. But his mind goes back instead to Zborowski and the Miller. In his own words, "it was when I was mechanic to Zborowski in the Miller in the first Grand Prix that ever had a mass start for, although the car itself was quite unsuitable, Lou was such an interesting being. For instance, he got the idea he'd be killed, which is not very amusing for the mechanic; but as it was to be a mass start everybody was convinced that there would be a pile-up that was going to be an all-time record. Everybody was in a state. It was arranged that Lou and I should go to a farmhouse right away from Lyons; this resulted in my walking Lou about at night discussing infinity and whether there was a God, because he was in such a state that there was no other way of dealing with him."

In the event, the Miller was even more unsuitable than either of its occupants could possibly have imagined and during the course of the race, over very rough roads, the front suspension and the steering completely disintegrated. At one point Zborowski shouted to Sammy, "steering's gone again"—and so they finally pulled into the pits once more and the hair-raising events which followed are well remembered by Sammy: "Zborowski began heaving five-gallon milk cans of fuel into the rear tank while I started to repair the shock absorbers. I say 'started' advisedly for, when I got to the front of the car, I nearly fell over with astonishment. The whole front axle had parted from its underslung spring on one side and was resting on the lower flange of the frame, while on the other side two badly bent bolts out of the floor were all that retained the thing in position. We had driven nearly a complete lap like that

Above: Sammy during record breaking with the Aston Martin at Brooklands track in 1922. Below: With a Morgan in 1930 at Montlhéry, taking records up to twenty-four hours with co-driver Gwenda Hawkes. Right: With Count Zborowski and the Miller.

and the axle might have come adrift at any minute. Zborowski quickly stopped creating a miniature Niagara at the back of the car and came to look. We felt rather sick and averted each other's eyes, each pretending his thoughts were very different from what they were. I had a long worrying try to get at the ends of the bolts, which had broken off flush, out of the axle pad, but it was only too plain that our Grand Prix had ended, loath as we were to admit it, but nothing short of a power drill could extract the broken pieces."

When it comes to the famous White House crash at Le Mans in 1927, which many of us would expect to be his number one memory, he takes a quite different view. It will be recalled that he came round the corner to find the road blocked with cars, but managed to slide into the melee sideways, and then to continue with a car which, although badly damaged, was able in the end to snatch the victory from the Aries. Was it a high spot?

Sammy says: "No, but there's an interesting thing about that White House

thing. In a way I owe the fact that the car was not wrecked to something that happened in the Grand Prix with Lou Zborowski. When we were going round the circuit we suddenly found the road littered with little white wood chippings; it was only when we went round the corner that we found a crashed Bugatti which had hit a fence from which it had made these little white flecks. At Le Mans I saw the same thing, and it registered for some reason. Those little white flecks rang a bell. So I didn't come round the corner at full throttle—mind you, it did not help much, but it helped a little. Experience suggested what to do—I wasn't controlling the situation; I wasn't thinking 'it would be better if you did that'; I wasn't thinking 'My god, this is horrible' or anything like that. But after I had hit the other wrecks and found out that George [Duller, in No. 2 Bentley] and What's-his-name [Callingham in No. 1] were all right, but it was their car I had hit, I thought, 'My god, we'll never be asked to drive by anyone ever again.' That was the main idea in my mind—there was

no suggestion of fright or what they call terror. It was a perfectly simple thing that I might have been sitting and watching myself. First of all, you have to remember that the whole thing was over in less than a fifth of a second, and what time do you have to get the Willie Whats-its then? Secondly, there was no time to make a decision—or at least to make a considered decision. But automatically my brain knew that if I could skid into the crash sideways instead of hitting it head on, I wouldn't damage the car so much—so I used the handbrake. Now the next part is simply due to the fact that I said to myself, 'remember last year'—and thought what the team would say if I didn't finish, so when I got back to the pits I kept everything in the dark as far as possible. If W.O. had ever known what was really wrong with the car he would have stopped us running, and I wasn't going to have that, and neither was Benjy."

The tale of Sammy and Dr. Benjafield and their heroic drive in a battered car is too well known for repetition, but this personal view does give humanity

Above: Sammy pouring oil into his three-liter Sunbeam during the 1925 running of the Twenty-Four Hours of Le Mans, which he and partner Chassagne finished second overall. Below: W.O. Bentley's boys in '27, from the left, F.C. Clement, L.G. Callingham, Baron d'Erlanger, George Duller, Sammy, J.D. Benjafield, W.O. standing behind at Duller's left. Right: Sammy at Le Mans 1927, with Benjafield and Bentley No. 3 before the race, and driving on to victory after the White House crash.

to the legend.

Other highlights in Sammy's memory are of a 500-mile race at Brooklands when he drove, as a last-minute arrangement, the huge so-called single-seater Bentley which used to leap feet off the track over the big bumps; and then, at the other end of the scale, record breaking with the tiny Austin Seven—a story which has overtones that go back to the very beginning of racing. "You remember when Edge did his first twenty-four-hour record just after the track opened—I was there by the way—he had little red lights placed round the edge of the course to help him keep on course in the dark. Well, we remembered that when we did the records with the little Austin, as although we were not going for twenty-four hours we should have to do some work in the dark. Trouble was that Edge had had headlights too, but the little Austin did not, and it was not funny driving round the circuit with only the red light guides. And the other thing that was so damn funny was that after I had been going for quite a time in the dark, I suddenly felt something soft and hairy come across my face—it blotted out all vision and then went away. I thought, 'well it can't be a bird, it can't be a bat.' I couldn't think what it was—and then it did it again. Then I thought, 'well if the underworld is going to take part in this record attempt it's time we stopped to consider who is in control'—and then the engine cut out. What had actually happened is this: In order to give us a long run without refueling, the Austin had had a second tank put in alongside the driver; it was secured in place by steel straps and these were padded with fiber strips. Now unbeknown to me, because it was dark and I couldn't see, it had come loose, and these fiber strips still screwed to the floor were wandering about in the air like an octopus doing Swedish drill, and one of them had come across my face. Finally of course the petrol pipe had broken, which is why the engine stopped. That was fun."

Other races which live strongly still in his mind are the Tourist Trophy events usually held in Northern Ireland; he has some particularly hilarious memories. One of them concerns a Singer. He crashed badly but, prior to that, this is the story in Sammy's inimitable words, beginning as usual somewhere in the middle and sorting itself out from there. "It was that Singer—I was told afterwards that we were leading—and by god it was going, that Singer—and you see, you come across one car, one of the team cars, upside down in the ditch and you think, 'oh well, I knew old so-and-so would make a muck of it one day.' Then you see the second team car in the ditch—two of them couldn't have made a mistake, could they? And then as I was going really fast on Bradshaw's Brae, I discovered why. The steering wheel didn't do anything. Well, that was very interesting, but again it wasn't frightening. I'd been told if anything like that happened to get my thighs from under the wheel, put one hand on the instrument board, one hand on the side, and go as sloppy as I could. And I did that. Well now, we went across the road and went right up on the bank and turned horizontally and then it went end for end and finished up in, I suppose what, a couple of feet of the spectators who were having a picnic tea. It was only when the car had hit the ground and I decided to roll out anyhow, that they jumped up and ran for it. They had seen the car pass as near as I am to you, but it hadn't registered."

Another story of great charm concerned the Riley. This was also in a TT on the Irish circuit, and this is how Sammy remembers it. "We came round the corner and there was John Cobb's car crashed, and John standing beside the

road and obviously all right; but in front of us, and this was quite a fast corner, Paddy, his mechanic, was creeping about on all fours in the middle of the road. My mechanic and I spent the rest of the race wondering what on earth he was doing, and we came to the conclusion that he must have hit his head badly and was not responsible for his actions. It wasn't until the race was finished that we learnt what was the trouble. Paddy had lost his detachable teeth—he never found them."

Sammy's last real race was with an Aston Martin at Le Mans in the early Thirties; but after that he went on in rallies and trials, and continued to run his tricycle Beelzebub in the Brighton run, until some time in the late Sixties when he was about eighty, which isn't a bad time to give up competition motoring anyway. Not that S.C.H.D. gives up anything easily; and when the Second World War broke out, he was off to join the Army notwithstanding any previous bad experiences. He was, to put it mildly, a bit overage; but as they only asked you to *say* how old you were, Sammy found this bit of bureaucracy no stumbling block at all.

His motoring and engineering experience was valuable and he soon had charge of one of the big mobile workshops—he still has a First Army shield above the front door of his flat in Guildford. The only problem came after the war was over, when demobilization was on an "oldest first" basis. The papers were not readily available, and poor Sammy was asked how old he was. He had to say he did not know, and when this produced an explosion of wrath from a responsible General, he had to amend the statement to admit that what he meant was that he couldn't remember how old he'd *said* he was when he joined up. The revelation of his true age did nothing to ease the situation. But as all they could do by that time was throw him out—throw him out they did . . . but not, one suspects, without a good deal of admiration.

Although he insists that everything today in motoring at least is as good as ever, he nonetheless has some fairly pungent things to say about the present-day racing scene, particularly when asked if he thinks he might enjoy it. "Oh yes, I'd enjoy racing today because these are the best racing cars that have ever been built by a long chalk—but they are also the most useless, and I would hate the circuits. I can't stand short circuits, that's one of the reasons I didn't really like Brooklands. I like the old-type circuits, if possible about twenty-four miles round, and I like the race to go on for hours."

There are, however, some attitudes today with which he really has no time whatsoever, and will tell you that he has seen reports of races where only the driver is mentioned—and the car isn't talked about at all. He still maintains that in any race it's the car that wins and claims that at any given time there are probably six people who could win any given race if they had the right car to do it in. He will then tell you he doesn't know what they are doing it for, which invites the question, what was he doing it for? "I did it to see if we could get some credit and some prestige for the cars I was driving. I wouldn't like it today with all those badges for cigarette companies. I wouldn't wear them, but of course they have to because it's the only way they can get the money. Anyway, as I've said, I wouldn't like the short circuits, and I'd had the idea that it was going to be the *driver* who won the race. I remember Coatalen saying, years ago, he wished to god there was some means by which he could get a car that would drive itself, because the drivers gave more trouble than any mechanical fault any car had ever had."

It is perhaps a situation best summed up in one of Sammy's own favorite poems, by Admiral Hopwood:

> In an age of swift invention it is frequently believed
> That the pressure on a button is as good as work achieved
> But the optimist inventor should remember if he can
> Though the instrument be perfect there are limits to the man.

There aren't many limits to Sammy Davis. ✛

Changing of the Guard-- A Lincoln

IT IS DONE. After decades as one of the world's largest automobiles, the Lincoln Continental has been made dramatically smaller, victim of a changing world. Even the big Lincoln couldn't hold out forever, a few years longer than Cadillac, perhaps, but not forever. Now an automotive era has ended, the conclusion commemorated by Lincoln itself which, during 1979, offered a special Collector's Series of beautifully appointed models. The very last big Lincoln of all was photographed as it left the line last June. It was rolled out sadly, surrounded by applauding workers apparently paying a final wistful tribute to a once endangered, now extinct species of the American dream.

With a new era unfolding, we journeyed to Detroit to see and drive some of the 1980 Lincoln prototypes, and talk with the people responsible for them. From their point of view, the big Lincoln and Mark V were tough acts to follow. Nor was the decision to downsize these majestic symbols of riches taken lightly. But the smaller models are interesting in a way which reflects a new awareness on the part of America's luxury car builders. Lincoln has stressed engineering when describing these automobiles and we kept this in mind when approaching the cars early last summer.

THE TEST TRACK & THE ENGINEERS

The handling portion of Ford Motor Company's test track is a 1.1-mile asphalt squiggle located, more or less, in the big facility's center. It seemed like an odd sort of place to introduce the new version of one of America's premier luxury cars. Still, that's where Lincoln had arranged for the very earliest drives by the automotive press. On hand were a Continental Town Car, a Mark VI two-door and its new-for-1980 companion, a four-door Mark, shimmering in a cloak of rose-like metallic.

Just for the sake of comparison, we took several turns around the track in a 1979 Lincoln, heaving it through the esses, awed by its silence, size, weight, and an understeering tendency that would not be denied. Pushed hard enough, the big car could be made to swing its ample tail like an overweight go-go girl, although it was clearly unhappy in this unseemly attitude.

But all in all, the big car wasn't that bad. It was a beautiful-looking thing, certainly capable of performing in the manner which satisfies Lincoln owners who are no more interested in fast cornering or neutral steering than is the suburban housewife serenely ensconced behind the three-pointed star of her sophisticated Mercedes-Benz.

From the '79 model, we stepped into a 1980 Continental Town Car, a prototype only since even the first trial production cars had not been built by early June. One is first impressed by the new car's spaciousness. Despite a ten-inch decrease in wheelbase—from 127.2 to 117.4—and a length diminished from 233 to 219.2 inches, the '80 has equalled or bettered the interior and trunk room of its predecessor. On the test track, the car's smaller size and over-900-pound weight reduction—to some 4030 pounds—are immediately evident. So too are its subtly stiffer ride, flatter

for the '80's

by Stan Grayson

cornering and quicker steering. The whole car's structure feels stiffer too, rather in the manner of a good European sedan. All this adds up to a car that can be rather fun to drive, at least on the smoothly surfaced track. How well poised it will be on real world roads remains to be seen but it's hard to think it won't represent an improvement there too.

Basis of this smaller, more nimble Lincoln of the Eighties was a development program which stressed engineering as much as luxury, increased fuel economy as much as style. From its standard Michelin tires, selected for their low rolling resistance, to a body which has twenty-two percent less drag than initial designs, the 1980 has a substantial dose of new and timely thinking.

Summing up the project, veteran engineer Steve Bussa said, "I think the outstanding thing is how well the cars compare with '79 in that they're equal to or superior in every respect plus they have substantial gains in fuel economy of thirty-five to forty percent."

An all-new four-speed automatic transmission with an overdrive fourth ratio is fundamental to this increased economy. The transmission is housed in a lightweight one-piece aluminum die-casting and uses a new type oil which reduces friction and enhances smoothness. Even on the Dearborn handling track, the transmission's smooth shifting was noticeable. It also has nonadjustable bands to reduce maintenance.

Coupled to this transmission is a standard fuel-injected engine, either a five-liter or the 351 Windsor. Both are equipped with the latest Lincoln-Mercury control system, EEC III, which uses an array of modules and sensors to control literally 100 percent of the engines' functions. "There is no connection," engineer Bussa pointed out, "between the accelerator pedal the driver pushes and the fuel going into the manifold. Response time is about one-third that of a normal carb system. The computer is actually faster than a direct linkage." Acceleration of the cars we drove felt decent. Rear axle ratios are mated to either of the two engines so that even with the standard 302, performance will be adequate. Those planning on trailer towing, of course, will want the 351.

The engine/transmission unit are mounted in a frame which is seventy-eight pounds lighter than its forerunner. Compared to the Mercury frame on which it is based, it has an additional front cross member and tubular K-braces from side rail to engine mounts to increase stiffness and decrease shake. At the rear, a new box section type design eliminates the need for a cross member there. Fitted to this sturdy frame are specially tuned rubber body mounts designed to isolate the body from noise and vibration. The new car is certainly as silent as the old.

The new steering gear relies on improved geometry and quicker ratios—14 to one, compared to 17 to one—to achieve substantial improvements over earlier models. It also has somewhat increased road feel. Suspension, front and rear, is new. At the front, the older model's arm and drag strut have been replaced by stamped upper and lower A-arms operating together with a short coil spring, stabilizer bar and permanently lubricated ball joints. The rear axle is located by four links with coil springs mounted atop the axle's center. The shocks are affixed just forward of these springs and are nearly vertical for maximum efficiency. All suspension bushings have been molded oversize to help

Towards 1980. Pictured here are styling studies for the new Lincoln. Some are rather evocative of Lagonda's latest sedan. During planning sessions, the

esigners considered elements of many classics. Some AUTOMOBILE Quarterly hotographs used for study are visible on the wall behind the full-scale model.

isolate suspension movement and noise from frame and body.

Since the suspension must now support rather less weight than in the past, all the components are lighter themselves, eighty pounds lighter to be exact. Sixty-four pounds have been pared from the brakes too, thanks largely to use of finned aluminum rear drums with iron liners and a high strength steel center section. Weight has also been saved by a simplified front disc brake caliper mounting arrangement.

So many new components meant a lot of testing even before the first prototype was completed sometime in the spring of 1978. By then, each individual piece had already passed lab tests before being installed on the first test chassis for durability testing on the road. How do the engineers decide when a part is durable enough?

Bussa: "It's essentially historical perspective. We have proving ground durability routes based on long experience. We've been using some since the 1940's. The routes and procedures have evolved over the years to where we have very high confidence."

According to Bussa and his colleagues, there were no particularly difficult aspects of the new Lincoln project although it did have its share of challenges. These challenges were met thanks in part to the first full-scale use at Lincoln of computer analysis. Among other things, the computers reduced the number of fender structures which needed to actually be built for testing from four to two. The Lincoln engineers seemed especially proud of the fact that the cars offer significant improvements in roadability while suffering no degradation in ride. The latter, they all know full well, remains among the most important factors of all to buyers of domestic luxury cars.

THE STYLING STUDIO & THE DESIGNERS

"One thing we did was a lot of research on some of the classics, gathered up a lot of photographs and tried to find some of the classic cues that could be incorporated into an all-new design." Gail Halderman, head of the 1980 Lincoln design team, was talking about the inception of the new car. We were sitting in his lovely office in Ford's corporate design center, a plush building decorated with healthy green plants and good modern art.

Although the designers started the Lincoln project with a clean sheet of paper, there was nothing simple about their task. While they may have had the freedom to create an all-new shape, the basic consideration was whether they really wanted one. How far to depart from an established and successful image? That was the question. Anyone familiar with the postwar development of Lincoln automobiles will recognize the problem. From 1949 through 1960 the company tried several different body styles and established no family lineage. Looking back, today's designers cite the slab-sided '61 as the forebear of the current Lincoln look.

"We tried some designs that had more flowing lines but felt this departed too far from the appearance we worked so hard to get," said Halderman, "especially on the Mark. We really took the Mark V and tried to modify it. . . . We thought it was an absolute must to not change the appearance or the overall look of the car from its current day established design . . . as a classic, good, expensive car. You don't want to destroy that in one year."

When Lincoln designers talk about the "Lincoln look," they mean what they think of as the car's "classic sheerness" and its elegant, formal-looking front and rear. In a very real sense, the new cars are somewhat smaller versions of the familiar Continental and Mark V. For the designers, the prime difficulty was shrinking the package while holding the interior dimensions. "It became so easy," Halderman recalls, "to make the car look over-roofed, and we struggled a bit with that." Even tougher was taking dimension out of the car without making it look stubby, short and chopped.

Bill Cramer, one of the eight or so designers who worked with Halderman saw the problem as avoiding an overly bloated look. "Keep it sheer. Keep it linear."

Having gone to all this trouble to create an impression of uninterrupted lines, it seemed odd that the designers included the familiar half-vinyl top option which does little but create a rather chopped, vertical look, the very thing the designers were trying to avoid.

"That's true," said one of them. "You know the half-vinyl tops do that to anything. On the Versailles it falls right out—stubby. It just happens that the older, longer, bigger cars accepted it a lot easier. Now because that's a very accepted method of making a Lincoln better than a Ford or Mercury, you have to go back and provide that." A full vinyl roof, however, is standard equipment.

All things considered, one can say that the 1980 Lincoln is basically a stylistic evolution rather than a break with traditional Lincoln looks. The immediately recognizable grille shell remains, now hinged to swing away on impact, topped with the familiar ornament. The fenders, A-pillars and doors hearken back to existing models although a lot of tooling was done on all edges and surfaces of the new car to reduce drag. A new vertical rear quarter light has been added to the Continental to enhance visibility while the four-door Mark gets the familiar oval opera window, a shape inspired by cars of the Twenties and Thirties.

On average the new smaller bodies—stampings for which continue to be made at the Budd Company—are 391 pounds lighter than previous models. Part of the savings derives from aluminum hood and trunk lids which operate on gas-filled struts rather than the more common torsion bar springs and save an additional 3.5 pounds. The bumpers too are aluminum although there remains some dissatisfaction with their appearance. Doors on the new models have been made thinner to save weight and are now mounted on tilted hinges which tends to make getting in and out easier in tight spaces.

The final configuration of the new Lincoln's seats was not decided upon at the time we drove the car. They look plush, of course, but the designers were still experimenting with various cushions. The interior is noteworthy for its feeling of spaciousness, front and rear. The Continental's instrument panel is straightforward and typical of American luxury cars, possessed of only a speedometer, fuel and temperature gauges and clock. Optional on the Continental and standard on the Mark VI is an electronic dashboard with digital speedometer, graphic fuel gauge and

412

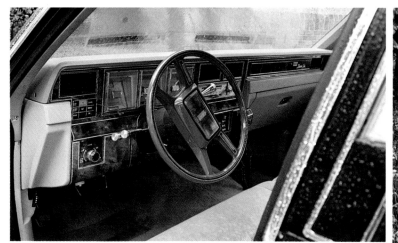

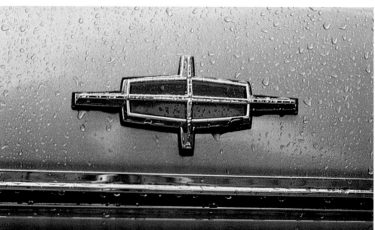

1980 Lincoln photographed at Cranbrook House, Bloomfield Hills, Michigan.

some dozen buttons enabling one to find distance 'til empty, fuel consumption, ETA, etc., all the things drivers have done without for presumably too long. The push of a button will now tell you the status of your car's various vital systems and indicate whether a door may be ajar or a light burned out. This vastly expensive new toy—as an option it will cost over $1000—is produced by Ford's aerospace division. It takes its place in a seemingly new craze by carbuilders for such electronic gizmos. Everyone from Lincoln to Lagonda is using them and wealthy drivers presumably are going to like them. The Lincoln even has electronic door locks. Touching the right combination of numbers on the door will unlock the car: Lincoln calls this a "keyless entry system."

Looking back at what he and his designers have wrought, Gail Halderman seems relatively satisfied. All involved in the project were aware of a certain tradition within the division and wanted to do nothing to change it. "We learned the hard way," said Halderman. "We would change the Lincoln back years ago, every year. Then we'd stand back and watch Cadillac do virtually nothing. They'd retool but keep the same look. We learned the hard way that you have to stay in there and just refine."

RENAISSANCE CENTER & THE PR MEN

The buildings, designed by architect John Portman of black-tinted glass, steel and concrete, tower up high over downtown Detroit. That they are there at all is largely the result of Henry Ford II's own vision and will. Here, Ford has moved from Dearborn many of its personnel and here, after a swift ride up a glass-enclosed elevator with its spectacular view, one finds the offices of Lincoln's public relations staff. From this vantage point, one can see barges moving up the Detroit River, laden with raw materials. Other barges move the opposite direction, carrying freight cars loaded with new automobiles to piers where tow boats—built with ungainly-looking high pilot houses so the helmsman can see over the cars—maneuver their charges into the docks.

In Renaissance Center, Lincoln's PR staff people are at work on a program that is, in some ways, as new as their offices. They are introducing a new Lincoln and talking not so much about luxury and style as about engineering and cruising range. They and the company's new ad agency, Young & Rubicam, are charged with convincing the public that, after all these years of selling bigger is better, for 1980 and beyond, smaller is better.

It should be pointed out too that there was some disagreement about this whole downsizing project within the company's highest echelons. Said one source: "Henry Ford was for the downsize but Lee Iacocca was not. The ad agency (then Kenyon and Eckhardt) was nervous. The marketing people were nervous. The dealers kept saying, 'You know, in Texas they like their big Lincolns.' "

By June 1979, with the smaller car a fact and with shortages of gas and higher fuel prices a reality, fears about the new car's acceptance were diminished. "People perceive the new Lincoln as somewhat smaller but still a large, comfortable, luxury-type automobile," said marketing man Tom Green. "The Lincoln and Mark cues of past years have been retained."

Increased fuel costs are not thought by Lincoln men to be much of a factor in their market. More important, says PR chief Ed Gorman, is the smaller car's increased range per tankful. "Availability is the important thing," he commented. "Too, nobody wants the stigma of being pointed out as driving a gas guzzler." The new Lincoln may have the very highest fuel economy ratings in the full-size luxury car class, 18-22 mpg.

On other important selling points, the new cars also figure to do very well. Lincoln's market research has revealed the following seven items as tops in priority among buyers of cars like the Continental and the Cadillac De Ville: riding comfort, well-made car, quietness, durability, reliability, seating capacity, luggage space and styling. Dealer service and value for money also are important and Lincolns have always done well here too.

Looking ahead to the '80 model year, Lincoln executives seem to feel Cadillac's Eldorado may have some advantages because of its front wheel drive, four wheel disc brakes, independent rear suspension and diesel engine option. But the Eldorado remains a smaller car than the Mark version Lincolns, has no four-door offering and nothing like the popular Mark designer series models. Compared to the '80 De Ville, Lincoln expects to have an advantage in nearly every area, from comfort to quality, the latter always a Lincoln strongpoint which should be even more so in '80 because of the increased emphasis on paint and trim at the Wixom assembly plant.

"We have researched [our cars] against the GM properties and the new Lincoln and Mark are winners hands down," says Tom Green.

Who buys cars like this? Lincoln's studies reveal that both Cadillac and Lincoln buyers share many things in common including median incomes of $36,000 to $37,000. Some seventy percent of Continental and De Ville buyers are forty-five or older with twenty-eight percent falling in the 25-44 age group. Buyers of Mark series Lincolns or Eldorados tend to be both younger and wealthier. For them, status and style seem to be truly significant. Lincoln even plans to use a slightly higher angle when photographing its Mark series cars because "our photographic research has shown that these angle differences increase the perceived product differentiation between the cars."

All the company's market research seems to have been accurate and sales techniques successful. The measure of the older cars' popularity is best reflected by the fact that, right up 'til the gas crunch of '79, the company simply couldn't build enough of them. The factory has been on a double shift for the last three years to meet demand. About mid-way through 1980, plans call for a slight production increase at Wixom to meet anticipated high demands for the new models too.

In a sense, the new Lincolns will reap the benefits of a luxury car market that has gained in strength even during difficult 1974 and 1975. "As more people earn $25,000 or more—which has always been an important sort of measure—the market grows," said Ed Gorman. Even with base prices of $12,000 for the Continental and $14,000 for the Mark, Gorman sees a strong market for the new Lincolns. It will be interesting to watch consumer reaction to these new automobiles. If corporate thinking is correct, the cars are arriving on the scene at precisely the right time.✤

The Fiery Genius of Mauro Forghieri

"Everything that I now am, all I've done in the past and will do in the future, I owe to Enzo Ferrari and his great confidence in me."

Mauro Forghieri

by Wim Oude Weernink

e has lived the Ferrari legend for over two decades. He began as a company apprentice and instructor, grew up as a designer, became technical director and today, at age forty-four, is a unique figure within the company he loves and the world of international motor racing. While men like John Cooper, Colin Chapman or Jack Brabham labored to create their own companies, he has devoted himself totally to the marque Ferrari. In doing so, Mauro Forghieri became the architect of Ferrari's revival, besides influencing the evolution of the modern racing automobile. Recently named a Cavaliere by the Italian government, Forghieri has for years been thought of as Ferrari's "technical Commendatore."

In a way, Mauro Forghieri's career with Ferrari started the moment he was born in 1935. At that time, his father worked for Scuderia Ferrari in Modena as chief toolmaker and miller. In fact, it was the senior Forghieri who machined the very first eight-cylinder engine casting for the Alfa Romeo 158. Although he worked in the Italian aircraft industry during World War II, Forghieri Sr. returned to Ferrari soon after the war. He was able to provide a comfortable home for his family and young Mauro received a good education, eventually graduating from Bologna University where he studied mechanical engineering and specialized in internal combustion engines. Forghieri refers to Bologna as a "typical Latin school" which stressed not only engineering but the liberal arts. He did his doctoral thesis on the Dyna Panhard as a small and economical car for the European "common market." The car's engine, an air-cooled, horizontally-opposed twin, especially fascinated him.

Forghieri successfully completed all his exams in 1959, uncertain of exactly what he wanted to do. In his heart, he wanted to become a specialist in gas turbine aircraft engines and made plans to study them in America. At the same time, his professor at Bologna offered Mauro a teaching post with the eventual prospect of a professorship. While Forghieri was considering these alternatives, Enzo Ferrari invited him—through Forghieri Sr.—to come to Maranello's training school to teach. With some reservations, Forghieri did so, little realizing at age twenty-five what the future at Ferrari held for him.

Soon after his hiring, Forghieri became involved in the calculations for engineer Carlo Chiti's 120° degree V-6 Formula One engine, a project on which he was supervised by Franco Rocchi. That engine powered Phil Hill to his 1961 World Championship. Of the winning Type 156, Forghieri says: "Nice to look at but aerodynamically speaking, not functional." Aerodynamics have always been a favorite subject of his. Not long after he joined Ferrari, Forghieri found himself in the ticklish situation of being left almost alone when the other engineers suddenly walked out after the 1961 season. He has always refused to discuss the politics surrounding that walkout but it is known that he and Chiti sometimes had differing opinions and that drivers didn't take kindly to young Forghieri's opinionated way.

Chiti says of the walkout: "I left Ferrari with other colleagues because of personal disagreements with the Commendatore, and not because of any problems at the technical level. After all, in the years before my departure, we won three world championships for constructors and two in Formula One. In 1959-1960, I got two young engineers, Forghieri and Dallara (who went to Maserati in 1961). Forghieri was then still at the start of his career, so his technical level at that stage was not yet so high that we could have real disagreements."

But the walkout had a profound effect on Forghieri's career. Whether or not Enzo Ferrari had planned to reorganize his racing department and replace the older people, he now named the twenty-seven-year-old Forghieri to be technical director of the racing department. Helping him would be engineers Rocchi, Salvarani, Marchetti and Zambelli. Among Forghieri's first tasks was improving the handling of the recently homologated GTO. Testing the first car, Willy Mairesse had a bad crash in the mountains outside Maranello, caused by the car's instability. Since the GTO had been homologated with coil springs and two reaction arms, there was nothing basic Forghieri could change. Instead, he chose to fit semi-elliptic springs while retaining the coils but making them very soft indeed. It was a modest success, a sidelight to the difficult 1962 racing program.

Carlo Chiti believes there is no reason Ferrari should have had such a difficult season in 1962. "I do not quite understand why Forghieri says he had to start from scratch. The car that scored the 1961 World Championship title for Phil Hill won eight out of ten GP's including the sensational 1-2-3-4 score at the Belgian GP. And when I parted with Ferrari, I had left a very progressive design, a car with a transverse-mounted aircooled V-8 of 1500 cc, a concept like the later Honda. But because of some jealousy, this design never materialized in 1962."

But Forghieri says of the 1962 season that "I started from point zero. . . . Although the car had won many races in 1961, it was not the right design. On difficult tracks the bad road manners were proven but it took me a year to spot the weak points, the roadholding and chassis stiffness." The team struggled through the 1962 season with cars little changed from 1961. Changes were made to the bodywork, a blunt nose to replace the pointed "nostril nose," for instance, and the engine was tried with many detail refinements and a gearbox mounted ahead of it, rather than behind, on some of the cars. The same basic car was still being used in 1963, although with Bosch direct fuel injection, again with little success other than John Surtees' win at the German Grand Prix.

Not long afterwards, in September, the first results of Forghieri's thinking turned up, the 156B, with a monocoque chassis, Lotus-like front suspension based on a rocker-type upper wishbone, a new six-speed gearbox and alloy rather than wire-spoke wheels. With that car, development accelerated and Swiss engine specialist Michael May was brought to Maranello to help with the fuel injection system on a freelance arrangement.

"I worked on a no cure, no pay basis," says May." I think I found some eight or ten more horsepower. I worked mostly with Rocchi and didn't have much to do with Forghieri. But I can remember that even in those days, he was a man of much theater."

While May was at work on improving the direct fuel injection system, new engines were also under development. Vittorio Jano, the great former Alfa Romeo chief designer and a Ferrari consultant, drew up a 1.5-liter V-8, and Rocchi helped work out the powerplant's details. Forghieri was working on another idea, one for a flat-twelve. While Forghieri is quick to point out that projects undertaken at Ferrari are all a team effort and that "nobody can claim something to have been born from his mind," he has a special feeling for the flat-twelve. "I worked on it as if it was my personal engine," he says in the loud voice he uses when he wants to convince somebody.

Development of the new twelve progressed while the new V-8 powered John Surtees to the 1964 World Championship. The twelve was planned for the 1965 season. It was a four main bearing unit equipped with Lucas indirect fuel injection—used for the first time at Ferrari—gear driven cams and rather bulky two valve cylinder heads. The engine was a stressed member of the chassis and, apart from the Honda, was probably the most powerful engine in Grand Prix racing at that time.

The car in which it was installed, the 1512, was a brilliant piece of work but its development was curtailed by the switch to the three-liter formula for 1966. Looking back on that first flat-twelve and the V-8, Forghieri remembers clearly a number of things that were learned. The twelve with its four coils and contact breaker points suffered ignition problems. Fuel injection provided a slight reduction in fuel consumption against high cost and complexity because of the small tolerances of the metering unit. Out of these difficulties came improved fuel injection systems and the Marelli Dinoplex transistorized ignition.

In addition to the Formula One program, sports car development was also important. "Nobody believed we could realize a mid-engine V-12 sports car or prototype," says Forghieri. "So our team designed the 250P and, you know, it was successful after all, thanks to a lot of cooperation between us and Surtees and Bandini. New aerodynamic features helped the car. The rollover bar was an integrated part of the car's shape. These aerodynamic ideas initially came from Vittorio Jano who proposed to test, with Richie Ginther, a vertical piece of sheet metal at the back of our sports cars in 1961. This started the whole aerodynamic revolution at Ferrari. You know, Jano was a great man who didn't have any mathematical knowledge obtained by study, but an enormous feeling, know-how and experience. I learned a lot from him."

How busy Forghieri and his associates were can be understood easily if one remembers that, in addition to all their racing car work, they also had some responsibility for the production cars. "In the Fifties, all Ferraris were competition cars more or less," says Forghieri. "But with the Super America and Europa GT, we started to build pure road cars with detuned competition engines. This led to exciting cars like the 250 GT and GTE. The technical racing department was in charge of designing some special road cars that led to the 250 Lusso, the 275 GTB and the Daytona."

The Dino 206 and 246 were inspired purely by the racing cars, at least in terms of general layout and styling. Pininfarina chose the shape of the P4 for the Dino GT. The P4 always has remained one of Forghieri's favorite designs. "That car did so well, you cannot imagine," he says. "After the P2 and P3, we had to make a car that would withstand the Ford opposition. And it did indeed. With its very clever 4.4 engine, it went as fast as the 7-liter Fords on normal tracks. As a result of much testing at Alfa Romeo's Balocco test track in 1966, the P4's handling was superior to anything else. That fantastic Daytona winning car in 1967 proved it with Chris Amon and Lorenzo Bandini. The only reason Ford won that year at Le Mans was because they were very strong in every respect. Never before had anyone been allowed to have extra practice sessions on race morning to qualify some drivers, either. . . ." When he talked about the Ford GT 40, Forghieri spoke loud and fast, eyes lighting up furiously. He never considered that car really within the rules in terms of body design. Once off the subject, however, he became calm once again, recalling other aspects of his life at Ferrari.

"The Sixties were busy years, full of disappointment and satisfaction at the same time. In between all the P2/3/4 work, we did the Dino as an exercise, a sort of formula car with sports car bodywork of fiberglass. I liked it very much. On the Nürburgring in 1966 we proved how fast this car really was. Remember, this little thing with 1600cc (the 166 Dino) led the race for a time, came in second against all the bigger machines and, above all, beat the Porsches. Nobody believed the car wasn't really a two-liter. Only after we protested ourselves to prove it was a 1.6 did they believe it!"

In the meantime, the new three-liter formula had begun and Ferrari thought he had the right engine on the shelf. The new 312 was based on the old 290 four-cam V-12. It was basically a sound car but a bit too heavy. For the early 1966 races, the 2.7-liter Dino engine was used. In this new 312, the monocoque was retained but the engine only partly served as a stressed chassis member. But the 1966 season was a mixed success for Ferrari. At the beginning, the 312 proved fast only on more open tracks; it was too heavy for the really twisty courses where the V-6 powered versions were used. The decision about which car to use for each race caused friction on the team, especially between Surtees and Dragoni. Surtees finally walked out at Le Mans that year.

"For me," says Forghieri, "John was a bit of a special driver. When he came to us in 1963, he already had motorcycle world championships in his pocket and behaved more or less like a Formula One champion. He had a strange approach to his work, but he drove very fast, in great style, and proved a good test driver. Only he and Graham Hill and Dan Gurney could stand up to Jimmy Clark on a race track.

Clockwise: At Modena in '63 with a Tipo 156 are (from the left) Mairesse, mechanic Vecchi, Forghieri, May, Surtees and, in suit, engineer Bussi. Giving directions at Maranello. Ickx pitstop at the Dutch GP, 1970. Smiling after Regazzoni's Monza win '70. With Enzo Ferrari at Monza in '71. Checking alignment with Surtees and string. Mechanic Julio Borsari stands in the car; John Wyer is looking on.

Formula One power. Above from left: Vittorio Jano's legacy to Ferrari, the successful but short-lived Tipo 158 that helped Surtees to his '64 crown. Forghieri's first, the 1512 of '64 which pointed the way to the future. The potent, flat 312B. Below, the ultimate V-12 of 1968, 48 valves and 412 hp.

However, John suffered one disadvantage: He wanted to do everything himself including team management. But I had good moments with John. I experienced a World Championship with him for the first time in my life."

Forghieri did not have much time to concern himself with Surtees' departure. Nor could he concentrate on engines alone by 1966. He had really become a general development manager, dealing with Formula One, sports cars and the newly set-up Formula Two program and Dino 166 sports car. If he wasn't at a Grand Prix race one weekend, he was at a Formula Two event. With so many responsibilities Forghieri found time to work only on the 312's handling rather than its weight and the car won only two races as Brabham took the World Championship.

For 1967, Rocchi developed hemispherical combustion chambers and three valves per cylinder for both Formula One and the P4. But the season was unsatisfactory and Ferrari also lost at Le Mans. Then Mike Parkes had a bad crash at Spa and, only a few weeks later, Bandini was killed at Monaco and everyone at Ferrari was struck hard by his loss.

"Losing Lorenzo, we experienced something very sad," remembers Forghieri. "Some very special aspects played a role: the sentimental reactions of the press, notably the Italian press, the fact that he was on such good terms with the mechanics—he had started as one himself—and that he had improved as a driver so much. He had been driving his best race ever at Monaco. He was so friendly too. It struck me very hard and I could not easily forget that race."

In the end, 1967 had been a worse season than 1966. Neither the Formula One nor Formula Two cars fulfilled their promise. Still, Forghieri had high hopes for 1968. He asked for and received more staff and, as sports car activity was stopped, had more chance to concentrate on Formula One. Then too, the young and talented Belgian, Jacky Ickx, joined the team. The 312 was lightened appreciably and power was upped fifteen percent. Perhaps most important of all, Ferrari started the aerodynamic revolution, fitting the 312 with a wing and using it at Spa. The next day, Brabham had a wing and a new era had begun. Ickx managed to win the French GP

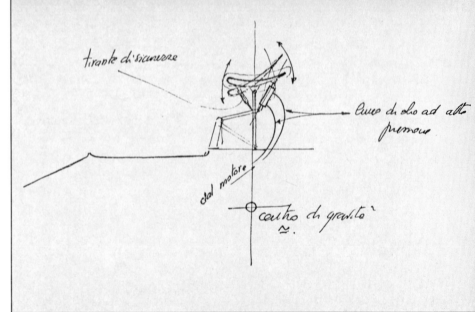

We are fortunate to be able to publish a couple of Mauro Forghieri's design sketches. Both happen to be of rather revolutionary devices. The drawing above is of a wing, hydraulically adjustable, mounted on the 1968 312. At once, the idea was adopted by others. Below is a 1974 sketch for the 312T and its distinctive intake.

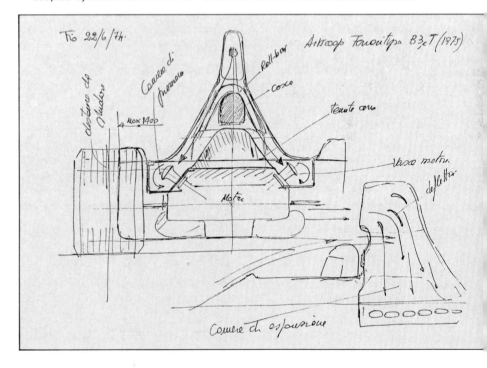

in the rain but his teammate Chris Amon was plagued by the bad luck that haunted his career. Otherwise, however, the 1968 season held little joy, the 312 proving rather unreliable. Tino Brambilla and Andrea De Adamich won the Argentine Formula Two series with the Dino but Forghieri was still criticized.

"For the first time since I had been working for Ferrari, everybody was critical of me. The Italian press blamed me for everything . . . One day they'd called me king, then let me drop—just like in the old Roman days. But when I am losing, that does not imply that I am bad."

Emotional expressions like that typify Forghieri's sensitive character. Why has he often met with opposition either from drivers or collaborators? Perhaps because he so believes in what he is doing and, while prepared to change his mind, won't do so in five minutes. On the contrary, he will search for technical solutions to prove his ideas correct. In doing so, he can seem quite conceited. Without giving the drivers any notice, he might change certain details right at race meetings. There he can be seen walking though the paddock, spectacles low on his nose, eyes speaking for themselves, furious, meditating, sometimes depressed. A genius at work. During such times, his hoarse but loud voice can be heard all over the Ferrari pit area, an Italian at his best! Only one thing makes him laugh in that situation, a win. Even then, he may be worried that something did not develop as he believed it should. With such dedication, is it any wonder that Forghieri is not easy for everyone to get along with?

"He can blow up and two seconds later, he is saying 'Sorry, I didn't mean that,' " remembers Ermano Cuoghi, the longtime Ferrari mechanic who accompanied Lauda to Brabham. "You forgive him because he is so good at his job. . . . He is absolutely objective on engineering. I enjoyed working with him because I learned a lot. And with Forghieri, you only learn."

Beset by criticism from all sides in 1968, Forghieri wasn't laughing. Upset, he suggested he resign but instead Ferrari asked him to stay and gave him complete freedom to design something completely new. At his request, Forghieri got five

Evolving designs: Forghieri's first visible change to a Ferrari was the blunt nose which replaced the "nostril nose" of the 156 in '62. Young Bandini, top left, in the rain at the 'Ring.

more engineers: Marchetti, an engine specialist; Maglioli, chassis; Panini, suspension; and two young men, Lugli and Piccagliari. He also got a new office, Uffice Study, in Modena. The idea was to bring Ferrari back to the top of Formula One.

Part and parcel of this effort was a reorganization of the whole racing department staff. Engineer Caleri and Mike Parkes got involved with the 330P sports car project using the 48-valve Formula One engine. Marelli was placed in charge of Formula Two and Jacoponi handled Formula One for 1969 with only a single car for Chris Amon as Ickx left for Brabham.

Meanwhile Forghieri went to work on his new car, thinking about it full time whether traveling, driving to work or relaxing with his stereo at home. It was easy for him to see that 1969 could be worse than 1968. The sports cars were much faster than their Porsche rivals but suffered the same engine problems as the Grand Prix cars. Formula Two didn't go well either. Amon managed only a third place at the Dutch GP and Forghieri advised Ferrari to stop the Formula One entry after the British GP. He wanted no distractions from his new idea.

Actual work on the new car began in November 1968. Every aspect was designed anew beginning with the engine. Again Forghieri chose a flat-twelve. But while his first such engine—the 1512—had been quite bulky, the new 312B engine was quite compact and narrow, despite its four valve cylinder heads and sideways facing inlet trumpets. Four main bearings were again used but with the end bearings now of the roller type. An engine similar to this appeared first as the 212TA in a 2469 cc hill climb car. At that time, an American airplane company expressed an interest in the engine because it was so compact.

The 312B chassis was originally conceived to be able to handle four wheel drive. This approach was finally deemed unnecessary, however, and by July 1969, the design was complete. In August, Chris Amon gave the car its first shakedown. By then, however, Amon was disenchanted with Ferrari. He hadn't won a single Grand Prix and he quit.

"That was a great pity," says Forghieri of Amon's departure. "He was so kind and we were such good friends. He had proven to be a great test driver and probably the best tire tester because of his sensitivity. Never did Ferrari have a driver with whom you could set up a car so easily. He was not lucky, for sure, but on the other hand, he was the first not to believe in himself. He always thought himself to be unlucky. Despite all that, he drove some great races, scored some magnificent sports car wins and only he could beat Jim Clark in 1967 and 1968. Unfortunately he remained unlucky with March and Matra as well, and I believe his decision to leave us was wrong."

Jacky Ickx's decision to return to Maranello with Amon's departure, however, was a good one. He joined a completely reorganized team which had the best mechanics available. Even so, things got off to a shaky start. The Formula One project suffered some delay because Ferrari also had to build fifty sports cars for the new 5000 cc formula. "The 512S was designed in no less than four months," says Forghieri. "That was too much. Internal problems at Maranello, strikes; all these delayed both the 512S and the 312B. The result was that I had to design the shape of the 512S in a hurry, which caused bad aerodynamics. . . ."

As a result of all these things, 312B development was slow. Still, after some early disappointments, Ickx gave a spirited drive at the French GP, outdoing Beltoise's Matra and raising everyone's hope for a win until he retired with a faulty circuit breaker. But his second place at the Dutch GP two weeks earlier really began a long list of successes for the 312B including wins by Ickx in Austria and Canada, and

Center: Scarfiotti in the new monocoque 156B with alloy wheels at Zandvoort in '63. Left below: 1512 at Mexico in '65. Above: Amon's 312, Monaco, '67.

Regazzoni's triumph in Italy. Ickx finished second to Jochen Rindt's Lotus in Championship points in 1970.

Ferrari was quick to realize the potential of the flat-twelve and started the PB sports car project under Rocchi's direction. While Forghieri went to the races, Rocchi became head of Uffice Study, concentrating on the PB's development and basing the car partly on the Dino 166/206 concept of a formula car with sports car bodywork. In order to improve the engine's serviceability, it was modified in detail and Forghieri had to redesign the B car partly because of these modifications. For 1971 the 312B appeared with inboard rear springs mounted atop the gearbox and actuated by rockers. Still, there were some big problems. Halfway through the season, the engines proved to have unreliable ignition and fuel systems and the handling of the Firestone tires was not up to par.

"Immediately the Italian press blamed me again," says Forghieri. "They said the peculiar rear suspension was a flop. Really it was the tires and the aerodynamics. When we made a new rear suspension towards the end of 1971, the car's handling did not improve."

Whether one could blame Forghieri for the disappointing results, or not, he this time became a victim of the critics and of an internal political struggle. When Fiat's Sandro Colombo arrived to take over as a result of the Ferrari-Fiat agreement, Forghieri was banned from the racing department in May 1972.

"I wasn't really 'banned,' " says Forghieri, "I just went back to my Uffice Study, now at Fiorano. I did not feel happy; I wanted to leave Ferrari again but the Commendatore asked me to stay, and gave me back my old job. I really got my old freedom in design back, without the responsibility of the racing itself."

Brian Redman who had been co-driver with Ickx in the PB remembers that Forghieri survived because "his status must have been very high indeed. He seemed very close to Enzo who passed his thoughts directly to us via Mauro."

Back at his drawing board, Mauro Forghieri worked out his new ideas of having a very compact and short car with a low polar moment of inertia and fully integrated aerodynamics. Thus was the T-car concept born. The first example was really the B3 "Snow Plow"—so called by the Italian press because of its shovel-like front spoiler—of 1973 even though its gearbox was not mounted in a transverse position. But the wheelbase was quite short and the car was rather fully bodied. At the same time, Colombo had another 312B3 built for Jacky Ickx at the factory resulting in what Forghieri calls "a basically good design which was put together in the wrong way."

With that car, Ickx and Merzario spent a miserable 1973 season. The car, the monocoque of which had been built in England by John Thompson, was modified in detail many times. There remained the question of which car to use for future developments, Colombo's or Forghieri's. Ickx found Forghieri's car faster but more difficult to handle and it was decided to develop the Colombo B3 despite its English-style long wheelbase and narrow bodywork.

"I chose Colombo's B3 for further development partly for publicity [he didn't want to risk a bad press by starting with his own new car] and also because I have a great respect for Colombo," says Forghieri. "The basic concept of his car was right. So in one month, I had put the B3 together in my way with the result that Merzario drove it to a very promising seventh place at Zeltweg. Typical were the new wide body with side-mounted radiators, the air scoop and integrated front wing, as on the original B3, all fitted to the Thompson-built monocoque." Three cars were built.

Towards the end of 1973, changes were made in the team's management again.

A formula car with sports car bodywork, the beautiful 166/206 Dino at Modena. Scarfiotti at work in the championship-winning 212E hill climb car of 1969. Opposite: Pondering the rear suspension of the unsuccessful 312B2 of 1971. The first wide body Ferrari, the B3 "snow plow" of '72. Ground effects and tiny springs, the T4 of '79.

Colombo left Ferrari for Magnetto Marelli and has remained friends with Forghieri. For political reasons, Jacky Ickx left the team. He was, says Forghieri, "a cool and talented driver with a good sense for a victory and—if well managed—a good test driver as well." Now Luca Montezemolo came in as the new team manager, one of Ferrari's best according to Forghieri. The organization began to work as a real team, each man playing a specific role. Vitally important, of course, was the arrival of Niki Lauda who would team with Clay Regazzoni.

The first tests of the 1974 version B3 were made by Regazzoni who broke the Fiorano lap record by a full second after only twenty laps at the new car's wheel. He and Lauda made a strong team that season and paved the way for 1975 and the 312T, the best-handling of that year's crop of Formula One cars with its transverse gearbox and efficient bodywork. (See AUTOMOBILE *Quarterly,* Volume XIV, Number 2.) Ferrari won the World Championship in 1975.

"Ferrari took the right decision by concentrating on Formula One only," says Forghieri. "I also succeeded in an old idea of having a strong team rather than a group of individual technical-thinking people."

A lot of new things were now in the pipeline. For 1976 a modified car, the T2, without airscoop—banned by the rules and reducing power some ten percent at first—and a De Dion rear end which "worked but we did not need it because the existing independent system was as good." Lauda suffered his bad Nürburgring crash that season but came back to win the title in 1977. Of Lauda says Forghieri: "When Niki came, he was young and learned a lot, probably more than during all preceding years. In 1975 and 1976 he was at his best, a constant and reliable driver with the ability to take advantage of a given situation. He was certainly a good test driver too, but he learned with us. After 1976, things changed; we had grown apart."

In his book, Lauda had a number of uncomplimentary things to say about Forghieri to which the engineer replies: "He accused me of half-truths. In Brazil in 1978, I asked Niki to stop all this gossiping . . . The principal problem was that Lauda, in his last Ferrari year, could not assimilate or be overshadowed."

In his book *My Years with Ferrari,* Lauda noted, "I do believe in Mauro Forghieri. This man is a genius. My bad luck is that I cannot get on with geniuses."

Forghieri found it easier to work with Clay Regazzoni although he missed in him the truly professional touch most other GP drivers had by the end of the Seventies. "He was like Bandini, close to the mechanics, a natural driver. But Regazzoni sometimes preferred the joy of life to racing."

Getting the opinions of others about Mauro Forghieri isn't easy. Not many people have known him closely or for long periods. One who has is photographer and Goodyear PR racing manager, Bernard Cahier. Says Cahier of Forghieri: "He is great, brilliant, talented and emotional above all. He has the ability to adapt himself to different environments and still achieve the best results. Over the years, I saw him growing better and better. When the team suffered serious problems, he came back stronger than ever. He can be humorous too. When the team suffered problems with its Michelin tires at Ricard in 1978, he asked me, with a smile, to arrange for a set of Goodyears. Above all, he likes everything beautiful, especially women. He loves them." One could compare him with a certain Gabriel Voisin . . .

About those Michelin tires, incidentally, Forghieri notes that "tires are the most important components of a modern racing car . . . the shoes of the car. . . . The developments certainly are not the easiest, yet we continue. The serious approach and very scientific knowledge of Ferrari and Michelin will guarantee success."

Another man who has known Forghieri for years and who has worked with him is

Henk Richten, a Dutch shock absorber specialist with Koni which has supplied Ferrari with shocks since the late Fifties when Prince Bernhard became friendly with the Commendatore. Richten knows Forghieri perhaps better than anyone, often working with him under high tension at the tracks on last minute suspension settings.

"In the beginning," says Richten, "he worked under some pressures, but soon after Chiti left, Forghieri formed his own opinions. He has his own way of working. He knows what he wants and is brilliant in many respects, especially regarding calculations. But certainly in his early days, he was very difficult to work with; he couldn't listen to somebody else's opinions. . . . Nowadays he is much more human. . . . Personally I rate him as high as Colin Chapman, even within the limits of being an employee, with Enzo Ferrari still making final decisions."

Forghieri is in essence a multi-talented man, capable in more areas than automobiles. He designed his own villa in Montala, the garden, even hydraulic pumps for water. For a friend, he might design a raincoat, create a painting or design jewelry. Of his own attitudes towards work, he says, "I always assume that everybody who is in the company with me will understand what I mean. I always feel that I am right and honest, because I believe in my work. Of course, I am not always

right. But again, I believe that I am doing things correctly and want to be respected."

Looking back on his years with Team Ferrari and Forghieri, Luca Montezemolo sums up the engineer like this: "Mauro was good to work with. He very quickly understood problems and how to solve them. He really is very intelligent, and enthusiastic at the same time. A modern-thinking engineer, I would say. . . . In his field he is the best, pushing hard, sometimes too hard. But that is better than not pushing at all."

After twenty years at Ferrari, Mauro Forghieri remains in love with the company. He has seen it mature and grow until it now stands as the most comprehensive such facility in motor racing, able to construct and test every aspect of a car with the help of its drawing offices, computers, research department, and able to rely further on both Pininfarina and Fiat. "Casting, machining, welding; everything we can do ourselves. You know, Ferrari is small, but the company is like a jewel."

And what of the old man behind all this? Forghieri's feelings for Enzo Ferrari will always be profound. "He gave me the opportunity to study, design and develop every component of the modern automobile," he says, "because he believed in me." That belief translated itself into some of the most beautiful, successful, and technically advanced racing cars of modern times. ⊕

Top: 1974/75 312T, chassis 018, the first of the series, used mostly for tests and practice. Owner: Frits Kroymans, Jr.

Left: 1969 512S Spyder, Ferrari's biggest engine. Owner: James W. Stollenwerk. Above: 1970 312B1. Owner: The Donington Collection.

1967 330P4, 0856, body by Drogo. Won Daytona, third at Le Mans. Owner: David A. Clarke. ● 1966 206SP Dino, 004, by Drogo. Second at 'Ring 1000. Owner: Dudley Mason-Styrron.

430

1964 330P, 0822, body by Fantuzzi. Third of three built. SEFAC car driven by Surtees/Bandini. Third Sebrin

rd Le Mans (dropped from lead by overheating), d.n.f. 'Ring (lost wheel). Lap record each circuit. Owner: Robert N. Dusek.

THE ELUSIVE BUCCIALI

THE NAME OF THOSE POETS OF FRONT-WHEEL DRIVE DESERVES NOT TO FALL INTO OBLIVION.

—J.A. Grégoire, in *50 Ans d'Automobile*

The name, in its native Italian, would be pronounced Boo-*cha*-lee. But having become French, by way of Corsica, it is pronounced B'yew-see-ah-lee, with uniform stress on all syllables. It is the name of one of the most breathtaking and esoteric of all classic marques.

The name generally is associated with the pioneering of front-wheel drive for passenger cars. That it is remembered at all is due almost entirely to one or two display chassis and a handful of apparently complete cars which constitute a uniquely phenomenal achievement within the classic idiom. The bare Bucciali chassis were downright seductive, but the cars. . . ! It is a matter of opinion whether or not they stopped short of being skillful caricatures, parodies of the super-long, low, show-stopping, crowd-stunning, concours Grand Prize winning creations which the greatest coachbuilders reserved for the chassis of the greatest manufacturers of the day. As attention-getters those wild Buccialis hardly could have been more successful.

The design of the more spectacular Bucciali bodies usually is attributed to the famous Parisian coachbuilding firms of Labourdette and Saoutchik. These, however, were merely the executors of designs which originated on a four-meter-long vertical drawing board in a modest shop building at 8, rue Gambetta in Courbevoie. There, on the banks of the Seine on the northwest outskirts of Paris, Paul-Albert Bucciali gave full-scale two-dimensional form to ideas which he already had conceived and sketched. There were armchairs in the large drafting room in which he and his brother Angelo spent countless hours, contemplating the work in progress and discussing how it should evolve. Angelo was the business manager of Bucciali Frères while Paul, the founder of the company, was responsible for product, in both its engineering and aesthetic aspects. He sometimes used the name of Paul, sometimes of Albert, sometimes of Paul-Albert, and at still other times of Albert-Paul. His friends called him Buc, pronounced *bewke*, and that is the name that I will use here.

Angelo was born in 1887 and Buc in 1889, both in the city of Arras in the *département* of the Pas-de-Calais, on the English Channel near the Belgian frontier. The paternal line of the family had been established on French soil long before the boys' grandfather, Laurent Bucciali, met and married a Russian girl. Laurent was one of the leading organists of his day, playing on such great instruments as that of Notre Dame de Paris. He was particularly noted for his talent at improvisation. And he taught the art of playing these awesome engines of sound.

His son, Joseph, followed in Laurent's footsteps, also becoming an outstanding musician, organist, and teacher. Beyond that, he also became a builder of large pipe organs and established himself in this activity at Boulogne-sur-Mer while Angelo and Buc still were very young. There they grew up learning their father's arts and crafts. Both boys were richly endowed with musical talent and both had a love of machinery which was abundantly nourished in their father's shop. I asked Buc of what his technical education had consisted.

"Can you imagine what it means to build a great organ?" he asked. "As a young man I built two of them with my own hands. It is a remarkable school for learning the principles of physics and of mechanics. And there is nothing like it for learning mechanical improvisation."

Later I had occasion to see a great organ dismantled for a complete overhaul. The pieces occupied most of the church's floor space and were almost bewildering in their variety.

Boulogne-sur-Mer during the first decade of this century was a marvelous city in which to grow up. As the leading fishing port of France it had been a wealthy center for centuries before it became a major sea resort, catering to the British as well as to the French tourist trade. As motor sports developed, Boulogne became famous for its races, above all for the Coupe des Voiturettes

BY GRIFFITH BORGESON

organized by the Parisian paper, *l'Auto*. Angelo and Buc became inflamed with automotive passion particularly for high performance cars. They followed faithfully both the French and British automotive press. While still in his teens, Buc landed a job as director of the orchestra at Paris' Palais de Glace, where the wealthy clientele tipped generously and he soon was able to afford, first of all, a one-cylinder De Dion-Bouton, then a two-cylinder Clément-Bayard, then a splendid four-cylinder, 40 hp Swiss Martini. He modified all of his cars' engines and coachwork to make them more racy and he dreamed of the day when he could build a car with a clutch on the rear axle and six four-bangers coupled end-to-end ahead of it. And part and parcel of this passion was one for the struggling young art of aeronautics.

In 1909, when Buc was twenty and Angelo twenty-two, Louis Blériot and Hubert Latham brought their monoplanes to Sangatte, about twenty miles from Boulogne, to make the first heavier-than-air attempt on the crossing of the Channel. The weather was vile and it took weeks for suitably calm atmospheric conditions to present themselves. During all this time the brothers haunted the Blériot and Latham/Antoinette camps, studying every detail of the wondrous flying machines and their engines. When Blériot did indeed make it across the Channel on that historic 25th of July, Buc made up his mind that he, too, would fly. He had learned enough to design his own Blériot-type plane. He tracked down and bought all of the necessary materials and built the delicate little craft himself. In 1912 he was able to buy and install a three-cylinder Anzani engine, whereupon he became one of the world's very early licensed pilots.

Buc took to flying as though born for it and began doing aerobatics during his first hours in the air. He was one of the very earliest stunt men to master the technique of looping and quickly found himself in demand at aviation meetings all over Europe. He became very affluent in a short time, since the standard payment for a looping exhibition then was about $1000, when bank clerks were working for less than $20 a month. He kept improving his plane and in 1913 his savings enabled him to become the Boulogne agent for Bédélia automobiles, the originators of the French cyclecar movement. In August of 1914 he was ready to sail for Brazil and an aerobatics engagement there when the First World War broke out. There were about 200 airplanes in all of France at that time and Buc immediately contacted the Ministry of War, volunteering his machine and services in the defense of his country. Both offers were accepted.

He began his military career teaching novice pilots in the famous flying school at Pau, former base of Wilbur Wright. He then did seven months of front-line reconnaissance at bloody Verdun. At Pau his knowledge of the Russian language had come to the attention of Prince Charles Radziwyl, who became a commander of the French escadrilles on the Russian front. At his request Buc was transferred there early in 1917 and he was on hand for the October Revolution. After that, covered with wounds and glory, including the *Croix de Guerre* with thirteen citations and the highest decorations of the Czarist government, Lt. Bucciali was routed back to France and into the famous Groupe des Cigognes. At war's end he was assigned to the aviation branch of the Ministry of War, where he played a part in the creation of France's first air-mail service, between Paris and Brussels. He left the army in 1920 to return to his old love, the automobile.

I learned all this in 1975 from the lips of Buc himself, and from documents which he made available to me. He had dropped out of public view over forty years previously but had been traced and found in the early Sixties by automotive historian William J. Lewis of Anaheim, California. Lewis, an outstanding authority on front-wheel drive, had exchanged some not unrewarding correspondence with Buc. Over ten years later he gave me the address with the hope that it still would be valid.

I encountered Buc, his wife Yvonne, and their daughter Josselyne in their attractive apartment in a nice neighborhood near the Champs de Mars, in Paris' 15th *arrondissement*. Mounted on wood at one end of the entry hall and looking like the piece of abstract art which it was, was a long rectangle of fabric from the fuselage of Buc's last SPAD; painted on it was the *cigogne*, the stork that was the totem of his escadrille. I had learned that there had been four escadrilles in the Groupe des Cigognes and that each used the stork in a different pose. The Guynemer stork, used by Hispano-Suiza with its legs somewhat raised, was shown with legs drooping and wings pointing straight down. The Fonck/Bucciali stork showed the bird elongated, taking the form of a sleek projectile. This of course was the emblem which Buc had used on the lengthy bonnets of some of his front-drive cars.

The ladies showed me into the salon, one end of which harbored the grand piano on which both father and daughter kept their touch in shape. The decor of this and of the adjoining dining room was dominated by an abundance of beautiful things—etchings, pastels, oils, small pieces of sculpture, all of them reflecting very refined taste. Two vivacious ladies lived here, but it was a masculine taste which set the tone.

Paul-Albert Bucciali entered the room, gripped my hand, and greeted me in a strong, youthful voice which belied his eighty-six years. The man was of lean build, about five feet six inches tall, white haired of course, and dressed in a plain gray suit. His physical movements were lively, his eyes sparkled, and so did his speech. In French we say that a person is *un homme délicieux,* doing him nothing but honor. Buc is one of the most delicious persons I have ever met.

Our first meeting took place one morning. It was supposed to have ended before noon but it lasted well into the night. I was enthralled the whole time, as was Josselyne, because her father chose to regale me with reminiscences, many of which she never heard before. Madame Bucciali had lived most of those experiences, too, and she helped to relive them. Affection flowed strongly within this little family group and the vibrations were of the best.

Buc's memory was vivid and sharp and he rarely had to hesitate to recall a detail. Everything he said was fascinating, whether it was about cars, aviation, music, personalities, or any other facet of his long and rich experience. It was all laced with wit and good nature. But one could not interview this charming raconteur. One could indicate an area of interest and then accept the stream-of-consciousness response. It was a rambling narrative which unfolded, in which nothing was come to grips with in a conclusive manner and which was peppered with statements of dubious exactitude. An important story to attempt to unravel was, for example, that of the most glamorous of Bucciali creations, the *Double Huit* or Double Eight, that magnificent V - or was it a U-16? But that unraveling was not to be.

I knew about as much about Bucciali as any well-read enthusiast when I was asked in 1969 to make a report to a prospective purchaser on the *Double Huit* chassis, then in a museum at, of all places, Lourdes. I had read the basic historical study on which most subsequent writing on the marque had relied heavily: the story by Serge Pozzoli and Gerard Crombac in *Autosport* (London) for January 18th and 25th, 1957. There, the 187,000 franc (about $7300 in 1930) chassis was compared favorably with that of the Bugatti Royale. It was "fitted with a sixteen-cylinder engine, built with Continental components upon a Buccialli-designed crankcase. The cylinder dimensions were 72 by 120 mm . . . one chassis was built and shown at the Salon, and was used on the road by the Bucciali brothers." But when I inspected the chassis it was obvious on close examination that it was merely a mock-up and no more capable of being driven than a cast-iron stove.

Going back to the contemporary literature one found the *Double Huit* listed in catalogues as an available model. But in the catalogues, aside from bore, stroke, displacement and horsepower figures, information on engines was consistently lacking. One had to turn to the contemporary motoring press if one wanted further details. The ultra-serious and authoritative *Automobile Engineer* (London) stated in 1930 that the big engine, "though it appears to consist of two vertical blocks, is actually a V-16 with the cylinders being bored at a slight angle within, including 22½°." *Automobile Topics* (New York) for December 27th, 1930 said, however, that the engine was a 45° V-16 of Buccialli manufacture. It added that one of these "may be seen at Indianapolis this year." But for detailed facts one could not beat *The Autocar* for October 10th, 1930, which really clarified the situation:

"First impression on examining the 'double eight' Buccialli is that it is a dual engine with the crankshafts united by gearing. This is incorrect, however, for although the two aluminium cylinder blocks are vertical, with a few inches between them, the cylinder barrels are at 22 degrees, and there is only one five-bearing crankshaft, which can be dropped from below without taking the engine out of the frame. The cylinder blocks have nitralloy liners. . . ."

How many Double Eights were there? Parisian expert Christian Huet, a friend of the Buccialli family and a student of the marque, told Bill Lewis that only two had been built. Buc let the question pass when Lewis posed it, merely remarking that the Sixteen "was a wonderful car." When I put the same question to Buc in 1975 he told me that three had been made—the mock-up, which was displayed at the showroom and at the Salons, plus two fully operational cars. This was important information and I wanted far more detail, but the subject was changed abruptly and it was a long time before I was able to introduce it again. Then I asked if his company had built these operational engines. Certainly it had. Had he used American Continental cylinder blocks, as some sources had reported? No, he said, but he had chosen Continental bore and stroke dimensions "for connecting-rod purposes." He told of running the Sixteen on a propellor-type test stand for twenty-four hours at a stretch, then—as was his habit—veered from the subject again.

Harrah's Automobile Collection acquired the mock-up chassis from Pozzoli, who had acquired it from Buc some time after writing his history of the marque. When the restorers in Reno lifted the rocker covers of the Double Eight they found, instead of nitralloy cylinders at 22½ or 45 degrees, that the "engine" was just a pair of sheet-aluminum boxes, full of old French

newspapers. Buc had *had* the world, including its technical experts, for forty years. Had he taken a torch to the mock-up he could have had it in perpetuity. But then no one ever would know how marvelously clever the whole *mise-en-scène* had been. As for any other Double Eights, Pozzoli/Crombac seem to have been correct when they stated that "one chassis was built." The best efforts of implacable collectors and researchers have failed to turn up even a fuzzy snapshot of another such machine.

As already noted, Buc was still working for the War Ministry when he decided in 1920 to build a personal car, strictly to his own taste. He designed a frame, which he had made, and dropped into it a three-liter Ballot 4J Sport engine, which was very similar to that of the very fast side-valve racing Sunbeams. It was smooth, flexible, and potent—and a *pot d'échappement* from a SPAD, he said, gave it a fine, booming exhaust note. He named it the BUC.

Building one fun car whetted Buc's appetite and confidence and he quit his good position in order to try to become a car manufacturer on a modest scale. Angelo was equally enthused and joined his brother in setting up the company called Bucciali Frères, builder of BUC cars at Courbevoie. It has been written that all this was facilitated by the brothers' "great wealth," derived from inheritance. Buc scoffed when I mentioned this and assured me that the little company was built the hard way.

Buc and Angelo became interested in the possibilities of the high-performance two-stroke engine and in the work of Violet, a prolific designer in that field. Their first joint venture was a racing voiturette powered by a 1340 cc Violet vertical twin having a roller-bearing crankshaft and a common combustion chamber for both cylinders. The brothers co-drove this machine in the Voiturette GP at Boulogne in 1922, in which Buc stated they finished third.

Although the names BUC and Bucciali appear nowhere in Edmond Cohin's *L'Historique de la Course Automobile* (Paris, 1966), the brothers evidently acquired sufficient confidence in the two-stroke principle to decide to found their line of production cars upon it. An old company document shows that in August of 1922 they raised 200,000 francs in capital ($16,220 at the time) for the financing of the new program. Out of this modest sum were to come the cost of the design and development of a 1496 cc V-4 Violet engine, the construction of a prototype car, its presentation and solicitation of dealers at the Salon that October and, finally, participation in the Tour de France of 1923.

The new passenger-car chassis was fitted with a rakishly sporting two-door sedan body of Buc's design. The car was called the AB4, presumably for "Automobile Bucciali number four." According to Pozzoli/Crombac, this car, fitted with the new V-4 engine, took part in the Tour de France "with no success." According to old company claims, however, the car was fitted with the unmodified engine from the racer which had run at Boulogne. Although the car weighed more than 3850 pounds, the claim continued, after almost 2500 gruelling miles the grotesquely underpowered car arrived *"en tête du classement général,"* in front overall.

The old racing car was super-light. Equipped with the new V-4 engine, which pulled 39 bhp at a sizzling 4500 rpm, it is said to have won the up-to-500-kilo (1100-pound) class in the 1923 Voiturette GP at Boulogne.

Whatever may have happened there, the V-4 was not a howling success and

435

Pictured here are several phases in the Buc story beginning in 1925 when a six-cylinder racing car struggled through the GP des Voiturettes held at Boulogne. Below the racer is a TAV8, circa 1929 with f.w.d. and a Continental straight-eight. The Bucciali brothers enjoyed a brief moment of glory when they opened a Champs-Elysées showroom next to Hispano's in 1930. The low-slung appearance of the ultimate Buccialis is apparent in a trio of photographs. Those below are of Paris show cars, the dark-painted one displayed in 1930, the other in '31. Above is the last Buc, TAV12 with Voisin engine and Saoutchik body.

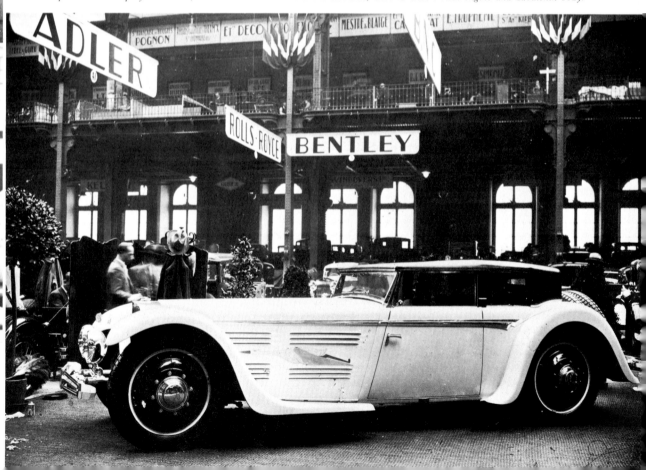

Violet went back to the drawing board. This time he tried an in-line four of the far-out double-bore type and of about 1100 cc displacement. A lighter prototype passenger car was built to receive it and was dubbed the AB5. It was no happier a solution than the AB4 had been, at which point Buc and Angelo bid adieu to Ing. Violet and the two-stroke principle for good.

Having gotten everything worked out but a viable power source, the brothers really were off and running, having no greater problem than to choose among the ample selection of good proprietary engines which then were available on the French market. Like many other builders of assembled cars they opted for one of the SCAP line, said to have been the rare single-overhead-camshaft model but more likely the less-costly 1616 cc pushrod four. This engine may have put out as much as 35 bhp and it gave a top speed of about 60 mph to what was named the Type AB5/4, also known as the AB4/5. Its quite conventional wagon-sprung chassis could be had with coupé, phaeton, sedan or van body—and at the price of 17,000 francs (about $795 in 1925), "including bare spare wheel," it found buyers. In addition to France, dealers presented themselves in Czechoslovakia, Germany and Spain, and Buc said that some 105 units were sold between the years 1925 and 1927. Unfortunately, not a single surviving specimen of this sole commercialized Bucciali-built motorcar has come to light.

Still believing in the promotional value of racing, Bucciali built a team of three slim single-seaters for voiturette competition. This model, called the *4 Spéciale*, probably was powered by the 67 by 105 mm, 1479 cc SCAP pushrod four and was fitted with an eccentric-vane supercharger. These cars must have served as test benches for French patent 573,440, filed in the name of Albert Bucciali on February 2nd, 1923, which I turned up in my own patent search. The object of this design was to avoid the wear problems associated with devices of this type when sucking fuel-air mixture; Buc's version compressed only air, blowing through the carburetor. He told me that the blowers used on these cars were made by his friend Cozette and that their weak point was very rapid vane wear. In any case this power package, which probably delivered less than 70 bhp, never was competitive.

At this time the ACF competition formula was changed to 1500 cc unblown, in an effort to break Talbot domination, and Buc took steps to compete in this prestigious category. He engaged the services of a remarkable engineer, Némorin Causan, a man of much talent and little luck who recently had done some good work for the Bignan marque. For Bucciali he drew up a seven-main-bearing s.o.h.c. six of 1459 cc which was capable of developing 70 bhp at 5000 rpm. According to Buc only one of these engines, called AB6, was installed in a *4 Spéciale*, which he himself drove at Montlhéry and San Sebastian. In his book, *Montlhéry, the Story of the Paris Autodrome, 1924-1960*, William Boddy mentions in passing that, in the inaugural GP in May 1925, "the six-cylinder Bucs were in continual trouble" and that Buc himself finished sixth, fifty-two laps behind the winner, a Talbot. Buc told me that the AB6 was basically an excellent engine which merely required development. However, he let it and racing drop because of more pressing new interests. For what it may be worth, it was two weeks after the GP de l'Ouverture at Montlhéry that the modern front-wheel-drive revolution was born on the Indy bricks, with all of its international repercussions.

This has not been an easy story to piece together up to this point but from now on it becomes infernally infested with error, contradiction, mystification, and sheer lack of meaningful information. The printed word, when available, has to be weighed with exquisite care. We have seen how misleading or misled the specialized press has been. Catalogue data frequently are deceptive or wrong and difficult to date. That reality can be approached at all is due largely to the indefatigable research and analysis of available material by Bill Lewis. Equally important are the company papers rescued, preserved and organized by two very distinguished collectors, America's Ray Jones and Germany's Uwe Hucke. The splendid libraries of the Museo dell'Automobile in Turin and of the National Motor Museum at Beaulieu have contributed some crucial documents. And then there are the sacred patents, each a solid rock of legal and technical testimony.

Buc told me it was in 1925 that he felt that something new and sensational was essential to spark the sales of his little marque, as a response to the overwhelming competition of the big mass producers, Citroën in particular. "I thought of front-wheel drive, of a car into which one would descend instead of mounting."

Buc would have it that he showed his first TAV's (for *Traction AVant*, front drive) in 1926, while Pozzoli/Crombac say this happened at the Paris Salon of 1927. It was in the archives of the Turin museum that I had the luck to find a copy of the Bucciali folder from the Salon of October 1926. It is, for all I know, the only copy in existence. Its cover reads:

> The Triumph of Automotive Technique in 1926
> The Bucciali Frères Car With Driven Front Wheels
> Independent Wheel Suspension and Double Steering
> The Perfect Pullman of the Road

Two types were offered, the 72 by 105, 1710 cc TAV Four Cylinder and the 61 by 85, 1987 cc TAV Eight Cylinder, both engines being pushrod SCAP's. A final note on the folder's cover fantasied. "Our 1,100 and 1,500 cc competition types, with front-wheel drive and independent suspension constitute the highest progress realized in racing cars up to this time." Such cavalier disregard of reality would prove to be a chronic trait.

Lending credence to the claim that the first Bucciali TAV exhibit took place at the 1926 Salon is a notice which is rubber-stamped on the face of this folder. It reads:

> At the Salon
> Ground-floor Balcony
> Stand 20
> (Under the stairway which leads to the buffet)

Small wonder that it was easily overlooked.

The cover of this folder is illustrated with a piece of artwork which is an almost exact reproduction, with the deletion of call-out numbers, of the head-on view of a motor vehicle which constitutes Figure 1 of French patent 639,393. Strangely, it was not applied for until January 17th, 1927. Also strangely, it was filed in the name of Angelo Bucciali and not of Buc. It was granted on March 10th, 1928.

It is titled *System of mounting driven front wheels for automobiles*. It shows a drum-shaped final-drive center section, on each side of which are pivoted trumpet-shaped half-axle housings, which terminate near the king pins. The king pins are tilted sharply inward at the top so that a projection of their axes intersects the wheel center lines at road level. The only internal detail shown is of a spherical universal joint on the king-pin axis which is integral with a stub axle in the wheel hub. The hub carrier is a marvelously complicated structure which is integral with the brake backing plate. Longitudinal leaf springs are provided as a springing medium but a transverse-leaf alternative also is specified. A highly characteristic feature of this design is a pair of parallelogram links which extend from the bottom of the central drum to the king-pin bases on either side, assuring strictly vertical movement of the front wheels.

Exactly the same dates apply to patent 639,394, also in Angelo's name. Its title is *Improvements to suspension and steering devices for front-wheel-drive automobiles*. It is much broader than its title would indicate and it can be regarded as Part Two of the original Bucciali f.w.d. patent. Among other things it shows the internal construction and contents of the drive line, from stubby driveshaft and pinion to the driving wheels. It shows cantilever front springs and a transverse leaf spring at the rear, with transverse parallelogram links. Two rather bizarre alternate systems of more or less Jacob's ladder linkage are shown for the steering. And, very interestingly, we are treated to a view of a combined final drive and change-speed gearbox. It is referred to as a variant but is the only one shown. It is transverse and bears the most striking resemblance to Harry Miller's U.S. patent 1,649,361, telescoping shafts and all. That patent was applied for on January 30th, 1925 and granted on November 15th, 1927.

Let it be noted at this point that French patents are "S.G.D.G.," which stands for *Sans Garantie du Gouvernement*. They are excellent for dating the registration of an idea but are totally unconcerned with prior art.

It would be some time, however, before such a Bucciali gearbox would see the light of day. The TAV1 had the usual flywheel-foremost engine arrangement, with a conventional (it is said) transmission between it and the final-drive drum. Something which was quite remarkable about it was its startling similarity to the prototype cars which Robert Dmitri Sensaud de Lavaud was to exhibit at the Paris Salon in 1927 and '28. The banjo front end, form of radiator, and cycle fenders all hinted strongly of the Spanish-born Franco-Russian engineer from Brazil.

However, and to compound the confusion, Pozzoli/Crombac stated explicitly that these cars were designed by one Edmond Massip. This has been repeated ever since and even improved upon by references to "the great engineer" of that name. As Buc told me the story, the TAV1 was strictly a Bucciali creation. I asked him about Massip and he told me the following:

"Massip was a very good draftsman, an excellent detailer. He also did some writing for the technical press under his own name and, to help his reputation, I caused his name to appear in print as a collaborator on the project. His work for us was completed in two or three months and when he left told everyone that he had designed the car."

In any case the car did not run . . . according to Grégoire. In fact, he wrote that it was not until 1930 that the brothers came up with a car that actually *would* run, which may be stretching the facts a bit. In his already cited book Grégoire wrote of the TAV1:

"Had this car been seen on the road its builders could claim the same priority as Tracta for being the world's first front-drive touring car. I recall that a Tracta participated in the Coupe de l'Armistice on November 11th, 1926."

I don't know how we can be sure that the TAV1 was *not* "seen on the road," but we do know that it was dropped. Transmission troubles have been mentioned as "the reason," and blamed on Massip. Our protagonists went to work on something better, which they presented in chassis form at the Salon of 1927. Said *The Autocar* for October 7th, "The six-cylinder Buc chassis is original and distinctive in everything but its engine, which is a normal side-valve model of 72 by 100 mm (2443 cc)." This engine appears to have been a CIME, another French proprietary make. *La Vie Automobile* for August 25th, 1927, in its haste to scoop its competitors, helped to confuse matters by illustrating its premature description of the new Bucciali with pictures of the old one. Both shared a stand at the Salon but the new Bucciali catalogue (which I also found in the Turin Museum library) was devoted to the new TAV2 and this time was lavish in the acknowledgements which it gave to Sensaud.

After praising his "scientific work" in general, the catalogue credited him as the holder of the patents for the car's springless, rubber-disc suspension system, for his "marvelous" automatic transmission, for his double-parallelogram steering which eliminated the conventional tie rod, and for his cast-aluminum wheels which incorporated cast-iron brake drums. In other words, many features which were to become Bucciali hallmarks originated with Sensaud. The Bucciali brothers took credit solely for their own patented drive to the front wheels by means of what they called "a double universal joint." Presumably, this referred to the axle half-shafts which were U-jointed at each end.

At some stage TAV1 appears to have been fitted with what has been called, incorrectly, "sliding pillar suspension on the lines of the Lancia." It was the just-mentioned Sensaud system of a vertical cylinder in which a piston moved against rubber pads or pucks which were intended to replace both springs and shock absorbers in a single swoop. This system now was adopted for the front end of TAV2, eliminating the previous cantilever springs. *The Automobile Engineer* stated: "The driven front axle is particularly ponderous and elaborate, giving each wheel independent movement. At each end, of the casing containing the de Lavaud gears is pivoted a large ball-ended tubular member made in one with the wheel hub. This member is formed with an upper arm projecting at about 60⁰, the end of which receives the eye of a rod on which are mounted rubber pads which form the suspension. . . . This is manufactured on the de Lavaud patents, but in this case, instead of the tubular casings containing the rubber being vertical, they are horizontal and actually formed in the transmission gear casing."

There were no "de Lavaud gears," the transmission being of the swash-plate type and a notorious energy waster. Buc's only reference to Sensaud during all of our time together was when he mentioned this transmission. I told him that Grégoire considered it to be a disaster and one of the two reasons for the ruin of André Citroën. Buc said that on the contrary it worked very well. He said that Sensaud, a very wealthy man, had spent a great deal of money publicizing this invention and that he, Buc, had fitted it to four or six cars in order to help promote it. Eventually, feeling that it still was not quite ready for production, he got on with his own transmission design.

Except for the transmission, with the TAV2 the die was cast for the definitive Bucciali system of front-wheel drive. Its chief particulars were covered in the famous—as we shall see—French patent 653,067, filed in the name of Paul-Albert Bucciali on October 4th, 1927. And let it be added here that it is to the greater glory of the original TAV2 show chassis that it, suitably elongated, appears to have served as the base for the majestic *Double Huit*.

Two Buccialis were on hand for the 1928 Salon. The only news seemed to be that while the Sensaud transmission had been retained in one car it had been replaced in the TAV2 chassis with a conventional three-speed gearbox.

La Vie Automobile for October 25th, 1929 presented the Bucciali TAV in its final general form. That is to say, with a set of change-speed gears incorporated transversely in a final-drive housing which also contained the ring and pinion gears and the differential. This unit and its articulated half-axle housings formed a mammoth piece of machinery which loomed ahead of the radiator and filled the space between the front wheels. It looked like some sort of heavy industrial vehicle from the front. From the firewall forward, the frame side-members tapered together to form a narrow fork which served as a cradle against which the engine, along with the entire power train, was bolted. This assembly could be detached quickly as a single module and replaced with a fresh unit if desired. This was a feature which Citroën would adopt for his *Traction Avant* and one which could have advantages in the truck and bus field. The all-rubber front suspension was supplemented by a sturdy, low transverse leaf spring. "Supplanted" might be the more accurate term, Sensaud's rubber pads now perhaps serving mainly as shock absorbers.

The change-speed gears were spur-cut and enormous, again looking fit for a husky bus or truck, as did the huge cast wheels, almost a meter in diameter and with 50-centimeter brake drums. Buc was particularly proud of his front-drive gear case and he told me: "Of all the front-drive gearboxes ever made, this is the only one, up to the present day, to have direct drive. All the others always have gears in mesh which whine. I put the ring and pinion gears just ahead of the clutch and attacking the gearbox, which made the change-speed gears turn about four times more slowly than normally. Critics like Charles Faroux agreed that something sensational had been achieved. Gear noise was reduced by an octave and you could change gears as though at idle."

Placing the change-speed gears on the high-torque side of the ring and pinion had been an aberrant peculiarity and the Achilles' heel of Harry Miller's system of front-wheel drive. In his patent Miller also had made utopian claims for ease of gear-shifting due to this feature. The reality was that the gears were virtually impossible to shift while the vehicle was in motion, and gear breakage was a plague. Perhaps this had something to do with the TAV's tank-like gear dimensions, although Buc's constant mesh on second and third, engaged by dog clutches, may have helped. I asked him if he was familiar with the Miller system and its problems and he said that he was not. I was surprised that this front-wheel-drive specialist had not talked shop with Gwenda Stewart and Douglas Hawkes during the years that they were living at Montlhéry and running for international records there with the so-called Derby f.w.d. Miller.

It was on August 6th, 1928, in the name of Albert-Paul Bucciali, that Buc

filed French patent 673,399, titled *Driving and steering axle, with independent wheels, for automotive vehicles*. It covers the gear case in detail and in this respect harks back to the similar gear case which Angelo had included in a patent a year and a half before. This new patent was granted on October 8th, 1929 and, with the previous one, covers Bucciali f.w.d. in mature form.

Bucciali's brief period of real grandeur began in 1929 with ever-more-imposing chassis and powerplants and with ever-sexier and more breathtaking coachwork, which sported some of the most prestigious names in the business. From this point onward there were constant references in company literature and the press to the cars being powered by "Mercedes SS supercharged" engines. Unfortunately for this thrilling claim the bore and stroke of the catalogued engine were given: 80 by 130. Anyone who knew anything about performance machinery would recognize the 3920 cc primordial blown Daimler-Merk of 1924, good for 70 bhp unblown, and for God's sake don't try for the 100 bhp that the blower could give for a few moments at a time. There was no excuse for trying to pass these relics off—and the brothers had gotten three of them—as 160/200 bhp SS's. Such misrepresentation could only have alienated the knowledgeable clientele, although at that time the brothers, like Grégoire, were looking to big industry as the ideal customer for their ideas.

The engines which did get used in the TAV's now were mainly Continentals—flatheads tarted up with false rocker covers. The connection was the great old racing driver Albert Guyot. Between 1924 and 1931 he was the small-scale constructor of racing and sports cars called Guyot *Spéciales*. He equipped his sports-touring models with Continental engines and became the agent in France for that product; Grégoire was among his clients. In 1928 he made a deal with the Bucciali brothers, who put their badge and script on the radiator and stone screen of one of Guyot's cars and sold it to a North African client as a Bucciali *Course*.

Another link with the USA and an all-important one was the brothers' involvement with Coldwell S. Johnston, which seems to have begun in 1928. Johnston described himself as "Former American Commercial Attaché, Europe, U.S. Govt.," and as a former export representative of Cord and Auburn cars. The L-29 Cord had focused international attention upon f.w.d. for the motoring public and Johnston availed himself of the American rights to what he chose to call Johnston-Bucciali Front Wheel Drive. He arrived in New York in time for the 1930 auto show in early January, accompanied by Angelo and Buc, and bringing with him a demonstration car. In a letter to manufacturers mimeographed on the stationary of the Park Central Hotel, Johnston invited them to study "our patents covering this famous construction which has been approved in Europe as the finest product ever engineered and produced." He added, "Writer has driven to Washington and submitted the car to the Bureau of Standards which are making a report on the wonderful road abilities of this car and the novel construction."

In an article placed in *Automobile Topics* for January 25th, 1930 it was pointed out that there was room in the Bucciali gearbox for as many as seven speeds, and other advantages of the design for bus and truck manufacturers were stressed. One perhaps recognized Johnston's prose style in such passages as "A. Paul Bucciali . . . is a former associate of the famous engineer Buggatti [sic], and has been engaged with front drive on his own account since 1920."

And, "In the model brought to the United States, an American Continental engine is installed. This was done to eliminate from consideration any question of the power plant by having characteristics which are known and recognized here. In the French cars a 100-horsepower six-cylinder Mercedes supercharged engine has been used, and with it, racing speeds have been attained and held for considerable distances over the National roads without any of the discomfort in riding, which would naturally be expected in such circumstances."

As the L-29 Cord had been introduced in 1929, so the TAV30 was introduced in 1930. It was a bumper year, for the Bucciali stand at the Paris Salon boasted, in addition to the tank-like Labourdette coupé which had been shown first in 1928, a handsome, brand-new Labourdette roadster and, of course, the spectacular *Double-Huit* display chassis.

In spite of the Mercedes name-dropping, such TAV30's and/or TAV8's as were built seem to have utilized a Continental straight-eight, the bore and stroke of which were given as 85.7 by 114.2 mm. This translates as 3⅜ by 4½ inches, the dimensions of the Continental which happened to be adopted on an exclusive basis by Peerless in 1929 and which had been used previously in a car built by the Case Threshing Machine Company. Peerless claimed 114 bhp from its 321 cubic inches but the real figure probably was closer to the 90 bhp which Packard announced for its eight of like displacement in 1930. Bucciali claimed 130 bhp.

The *Double Huit*'s dimensions were given as 73 by 120. The equivalent bore of 2⅞ inches was indeed one used by Continental. But the stroke, falling between 4-23/32 and 4-47/64, corresponded to no stroke ever used in the English-speaking world.

The output of the sixteen was first announced as being 170 bhp, but this soon was revised down to 155. Instead of questioning the greatly exaggerated power claimed for the eight, automotive writers enthusiastically made excuses for the modest output of the nonexistent sixteen, citing its smoothness and torque.

One of the best technical descriptions in the literature of the marque is in *Automotive Industries* (New York) for January 18th, 1930, and is from the pen of the highly respected P.M. Heldt. He presumably had the opportunity of interviewing Johnston and the brothers. He reported that "the Bucciali uses a Mercedes Type SS six-cylinder engine with supercharger."

A catalogue of the period specifies the four-liter supercharged Mercedes Six. It includes a side elevation of a huge racing car with an engine which clearly is supposed to be a supercharged eight. Except for a label which reads "BUCCIALI Type T.A.V. 30," there is no other reference to this design in the catalogue. It is presumably the basis for the legend of a projected Bucciali Grand Prix car. The drawing in the catalogue turns out to be one of those used in French patent 697,974, filed in the name of Albert-Paul Bucciali on October 2nd, 1929. Its title is *Coupling method and gear-change for automobiles and other applications*. A plan view shows that this engine was intended to be a sixteen, with two parallel and vertical blocks. A detail drawing shows two crankshafts, each terminating in a pinion which engages the teeth of a very special double-faced ring gear. This is not to be confused with a still-different type of double ring gear which was unclear even to Heldt and which was shown in a drawing on page 21 of *Le Monde Automobile* for April 19th, 1929. It shows a herringbone ring gear. A drawing on page 633 of *La Vie Automobile*

for November 25th, 1928 shows a similar arrangement except that the inner, left-hand teeth do not line up with the outer, right-hand teeth, so that there must be separate inner and outer ring gears. Or were supposed to be.

Concerning coachwork, when Henri Labourdette's *La Carrosserie Française* appeared some years ago, many readers were surprised and disappointed by the unexplained omission of Bucciali from that fine tome. At a later date Christian Huet wrote to Ray Jones:

"By the way, concerning Labourdette, he is not Henri Labourdette who made many body designs from 1900 to 1950, but 'our' Labourdette is another coachbuilder with the same name who worked from 1920 to 1930, and in particular for Mr. Bucciali."

Coldwell Johnston returned to New York at the end of 1930, in time for auto show week there. He brought with him a mechanical display of the Bucciali front end, which was exhibited at the Commodore Hotel, and another Continental-powered demonstration car. An article in *Automobile Topics* for December 27th announced this, reran its previous description of the unique front-drive system, and added:

"Capacity of the Bucciali factory is about 300 to 400 cars a year. Bucciali Frères has been in operation only about five years and previously had confined its production to racing cars, of which it has made 40 to 50 a year."

The object of Johnston's promotional work was to sell the rights to Bucciali front-wheel drive to one or more American manufacturers. In this he was not successful. Peerless did take a car and "the Ruxton company," which had its involvements with Peerless, is said to have taken another, for study and evaluation. Under what financial terms these transactions took place we do not know. When I asked Serge Pozzoli how the brothers could have afforded the high-rent showroom which they had at least briefly in the Champs Elysées, next door to Hispano-Suiza, he said that was where they operated as Peerless dealers.

For 1931 the brothers published their most elaborate catalogue of all: twelve glossy 9 by 12-inch pages in a silver cardboard cover. Six body styles were illustrated. There were artist's renderings of a two-door and a four-door cabriolet and of a Victoria coupé, all of which were very sleek and graceful. There were two boxy and graceless sedans and a roadster the stern of which was just badly conceived. All of the body styles but the roadster were characterized by wheel-hugging front fenders which incorporated a portion of vestigial runningboard, or so the form might be described. The roadster was shown with a cycle-type of front fender which encircled, closely, about 190 degrees of the tire. One of these bodies was built but fitted with the other type of front fender. It came out looking bizarre but amateurish, and it got very little exposure; only two snapshots of it seem to have survived. Also executed, and with vastly more refinement, taste, and success, was a two-door cabriolet.

While the roadster seemed to have the *Cigogne* embossed in the side panels of its bonnet and framed above and below by horizontal louvers, the elongated bird was carried out on the cabriolet in applied gold and silver sheet metal. A transcendental exercise in classic automotive opulence, the car was almost too fantastic to be credible. Saoutchik was credited as the coachbuilder and whoever formed the panels did an admirable job. But I think that we do see here the flowering of Buc as an automotive architect capable of working masterfully on

La 7 HP. 5 - - Sport.

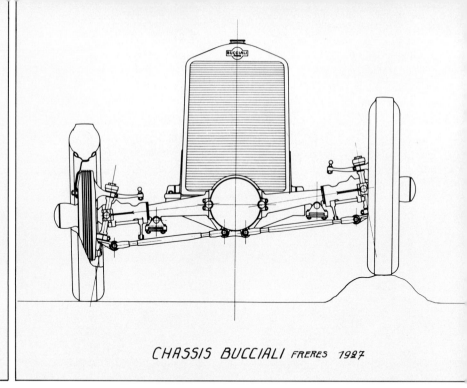

CHASSIS BUCCIALI FRERES 1927

Above, drawings for two Buccialis. The sketch at left was done in 1920. There is no proof that such a car was actually built although Bucciali did build himself a Ballot-powered car at about the same time. Buc was very proud of the independent front suspension introduced with his first TAV in 1927 and depicted its virtues in the drawing at right. Below are two of Buc's patent drawings as filed in 1928. The novel Bucciali cycle fenders and low chassis frame are readily seen. So are the intricacies of the front wheel drive hub and its universal joint.

Opposite above, the internals of the Bucciali TAV2 gearbox and the gearbox/engine unit. The highly-finished chassis were used for auto show display. Visitors studied details like the front axle and Continental six with an engine-turned valve cover. The TAV2 chassis appears at the extreme right before its engine was replaced by the mock-up sixteen-cylinder which Bucciali had photographed from above the rear quarter for use in a 1931 catalogue. It is now at Harrah's. Two versions of Bucciali's letterhead are reproduced. Courbevoie was the "works" address.

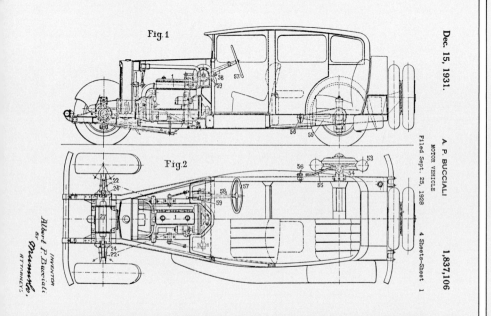

Dec. 15, 1931.

A. P. BUCCIALI
MOTOR VEHICLE
Filed Sept. 25, 1928   4 Sheets-Sheet 1

1,837,106

Fig.1

Fig.2

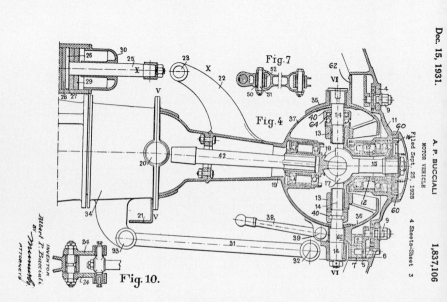

Dec. 15, 1931.

A. P. BUCCIALI
MOTOR VEHICLE
Filed Sept. 25, 1928   4 Sheets-Sheet 3

1,837,106

Fig.7

Fig.4

Fig. 10.

the borderline of fantasy. Nor would I be surprised to learn that Angelo's artistic soul also found expression in this design. The car's *raison d'être* was to draw attention, attention to the system of front-wheel drive that was looking for a big-time buyer. That nobody bought at that grim moment in financial history does not mean that everybody, from the President of the Republic on down, did not spend long, pensive moments at the Bucciali stand. The fact that no coachbuilder is credited with the catalogue designs supports the thesis that they were not done on the outside.

The following year, 1932, saw the presentation at the Salon of the last and probably the most gorgeous of all the front-wheel drive Buccialis, the TAV12. It was a hard-top version of the four-door cabriolet which had been proposed in the 1931 catalogue. Its powerplant was a Voisin V-12 for which 180 bhp was claimed, another gross exaggeration. Again, credit for the coachwork was given to Saoutchik and this time the bright trim around the fender edges—a hallmark of that house—was not omitted.

Collector Ray Jones found the car in pieces—or at least the more important pieces of the car—many years later, as he did the TAV8 roadster now owned by Uwe Hucke. Restoration of the latter is almost complete, while that of the TAV12 still is very much in progress. These two machines, along with the chassis in Harrah's Automobile Collection, constitute the known surviving Bucciali rolling stock.

In his very extensive research on the marque, Hucke has found someone who once drove a TAV Bucciali and who reports that it was a rather rough experience. In my own research on the subject I have not encountered the concept of the constant-velocity universal joint, although in some of the patents there is reference to the optional use of a "spherical" U-joint, which may be a veiled reference to the Tracta joint. J.A. Grégoire states that he never met the Bucciali brothers, which must have taken some doing on the part of all three of these front-wheel drive pioneers. Their shops were within walking distance of each other, both were getting their engines from Albert Guyot, and they were exhibitors at the same shows. In our discussions Buc was not interested in talking about "these people who cover themselves with flowers and only find fault with others."

Finally, I have not included a data table in this study because the data are so often missing, contradictory or inexact. For instance, how many TAV's were made? According to Buc there were thirty-six, while according to Christian Huet, an expert, there were seventeen. And the entire story is like that.

Not that it ends there. In 1934 the brothers began a project for a very exciting-looking four-wheel-drive sports coupé, to be powered by the Causan engine, by this time rather long in the tooth. This line of experimentation was dropped, apparently having led directly to what became a years-long project devoted to the design and development of a new type of AFV or armored fighting vehicle. Buc regarded the tanks of the period as being little more than armored truck chassis and woefully obsolete. His idea was to create "a very powerful, multi-wheeled cavalry automobile." It would have a top speed of about 60 mph on the road and would be very fast and maneuverable over irregular terrain. It was to be to the tank what the pursuit plane is to the bomber, in Buc's words. It was to have two powerful engines, with complete controls at either end of the twelve-wheeled vehicle.

In 1937 well-placed friends in government advised the brothers that the AFV was too complicated a project to be pursued further by them but suggested gas generators for motor vehicles as a Coming Thing, like war. Buc acted on this advice, first of all creating a *gazogène* system which worked quite well on the slow combustion of charcoal. Then, because the characteristics of the gas produced by such devices always are somewhat variable, Buc designed an instrument-panel control for the regulation of the gas-air mixture. He recalled that there was a moment early in the war when Bucciali Frères was to receive a contract for the conversion of *all* French army trucks to this patented system, which would have been a very important contract indeed. The German occupation is blamed for the end of that dream. Buc took his family to the south of France, where he spent the rest of the war years as the *gazogène* expert of the *département* of the Tarn. During the war his parents were killed and the family property at Boulogne-sur-Mer destroyed in an Allied bombing raid.

Angelo died in 1946 and Buc returned to Paris, where he worked on patents, first for the design of a light helicopter, then for an automotive gas turbine. These were merely part-time projects and to earn his living Buc took a position as general manager of Cotal, manufacturer of famous electro-magnetic transmissions. Its owner and the ruling power over its engineering activities was none other than Charlie Weymann, of coachwork and other fame. The company had not kept up with the times and was in financial distress. A major cause of this was the fortune which had been spent on a fruitless search for a practicable method of rendering the basic Cotal box automatic. Buc devoted his attention to the problem and came up with a solution that was remarkably simple and did not require the addition of a single moving part. It consisted of causing the speed indicator of any speedometer to trigger shifts by acting upon a light receptor—like a photoelectric cell—as it moved up or down the speed scale. It lent itself perfectly to the magnetically operated gearbox, with its electrically operated clutch. This "Transismatic" transistorized transmission could be rendered manual at any time by the mere touch of a button, and was patented in the name of Paul-Albert, who formed the Société de Mécanique et des Brevets Bucciali, which bought the Cotal company. A 1957 advertisement forthrightly hails the Transismatic as "The Automotive Revolution of the Mid-century."

Buc's creativity has not been richly rewarded. He told me that Citroën had lifted his ideas for the *Traction Avant*. He felt that the Type EBR Panhard et Levassor AFV profited irregularly from his own AFV. He told me that "the present Renault automatic transmission is based upon my principles." But the most bitter disappointment of all was the litigation which had been going on for twenty-two years at the time of our encounters. It was Madame Bucciali who took this most to heart, who urged that the "scandalous" affair be included in this study, and who kept directing the conversation to this subject. All of the family's resources had been poured into this fight, she told me, and all that they had achieved was the right to spend more money in yet other legal adventures.

A FRENCH INVENTOR PATENTED THE JEEP IN 1931: HE DEMANDS 350 MILLIONS IN INDEMNITY. This $63 million headline introduced a feature article in the important Parisian Daily, *l'Aurore*, for December 19th, 1965. After having been described as "the father of the Jeep," Buc was quoted thus: "I affirm, without going into the technical details, that it concerns a system of mounting driven and steered front wheels. It gave to the vehicle that flexibility and the adaptability to the terrain which is so admirable in the Jeeps. It is the veritable secret which permitted them to triumph everywhere and to become that vehicle which is indispensible for war, as for peace. Consequently, I am the inventor.''

Following the invasion of France by the Allies on June 6th, 1944, Buc observed that American-built military vehicles, notably the Jeep, employed ideas which he had patented many years before. He had granted no license for their exploitation. Checking, he learned that, during the war, the U.S. government had set up a mechanism for the emergency use of patents held by foreign nationals. This mechanism was called the Office of Alien Property and it functioned as a trustee for income provided for in license contracts, when and where they existed. Because no license had been granted for the use of Buc's patent, no such funds had been collected by the Office of Alien Property on his behalf.

In the case of France, where there had been many collaborators with the enemy before and during the Occupation, the American government preferred that the French government should dispense such funds owed to its nationals according to its own judgment. Therefore on May 28th, 1946 an accord to this effect was signed by the two countries. From that date forward it was France which held the pursestrings in such matters. I report these data as they appear in Buc's legal file and I cannot vouch for their accuracy. I encountered no clear definition of the status of patents which had been expropriated or otherwise used without license. If it were true that his patented ideas had been infringed or exploited, then he certainly deserved reasonable compensation. Seeking this, he filed a claim with the French Ministry of Industry and Commerce on July 21st, 1948.

Buc told me that the patent upon which the whole issue depends is U.S. 1,837,106. This is the American version of French patent 653,067, which covers certain features of the TAV2 front end. The American patent was applied for in the name of Albert Paul Bucciali on September 25th, 1928, and may reflect the beginnings of his association with Coldwell Johnston. Buc also provided me with a copy of an eleven-page single-spaced deposition made by his attorney to the French Council of State in August of 1958. It reviews the history of the case up to that time.

It begins with the usual listing of the plaintiff's virtues, then states that Buccialis ''were the first modern front-drive cars'' and that they were regularly exhibited at French and foreign shows from 1925 through 1935. It speaks of ''one of his basic inventions, that of front-wheel drive by means of powered and steered wheels . . .'' It says that ''. . . all of the vehicles of the Allied armies made in the USA and Canada were equipped with the device covered by his patent.'' It quotes a letter from the American Automobile Association to Buc as the authority for the contention ''that his patents were used in connection with wartime production of a minimum of 15,611,054 vehicles.'' Any government interested in not dispensing scores of millions of dollars would have been very prudent with such an adversary.

Following Buc's initiative in 1948 the legal body concerned had assigned an expert to the case. He found that the patent in question ''constituted an innovation in 1931, that the axles of the American vehicles which were submitted to him are a copy of the Bucciali axle covered by the patent and that infringement is obvious.''

For a moment it looked like an open-and-shut case, but the government fought back and the case was referred to a higher court. On November 16th, 1953 a new expertise was ordered, of two Jeeps and of two Bucciali cars. One wonders which ones they could have been. The experts' report was filed on June 14th, 1954 and it read, ''The Bucciali-type front axle . . . was faithfully copied by all American constructors who built vehicles intended for the American and Allied armies.'' One is constantly amazed by such sweeping pontifications.

Another expertise was ordered, always at the plaintiff's expense, one assumes. Filed on July 7th, 1955, it read: ''These experts both agreed upon the utilization of the Bucciali patent and established that the number of axles fabricated for war production, in virtue of this patent, came to 18,733,264.''

Then came another investigation by experts, whose report was filed on March 10th, 1958. Here it became clear *for the first time* that only two out of the eleven claims covered by the patent were involved, and one of them only partially so. On the strength of this the experts calculated that Buc was entitled to an indemnity of over 28 billion francs of the day. Buc's attorney referred to this as ''the indemnity owed by the U.S. government.''

The French Treasury department at this point ruled that no settlement would be possible without checking certain legal aspects of American patent law. Buc's willingness to settle out of court was not accepted and in 1965 he went back into active litigation. His position was not as solid as the experts had made it appear to be. A whole potential legal battle could be mounted over whether he had waited too long before registering his claim. The fact that he had sold and repurchased the rights to his patent during the period of litigation may not have helped. And then, *l'Aurore* concluded:

''. . . American law requires that the patent must be in all respects similar to the fabricated article. It is necessary that the Patent Office recognize that all the elements of the patent, without exception, have been used. In France, an analogy is sufficient. In the United States an exact identity is required, which is not the case.

''French law? American law? On that choice hang 350 million francs.''

It took a great deal of patience before anyone could find out just what it was that had been so faithfully copied. Claims 1 and 3 of the patent narrowed it down to the ball-joint mounting of driven and steered wheels, described in language which is almost impenetrably opaque. Perhaps the first thing to have done would have been to have determined whether infringement had taken place according to American law. Perhaps this patent, like so many others, had been circumvented legally, in which case everybody could go fishing. If the patent did turn out to stick in the USA, then it would seem that the USA should be the battleground, without taking on the French government as adversary. If the patent stuck there should be no question about indemnity, which could be handled through the Franco-American agreement.

It was a glorious trip and a tremendous experience to have lived. It didn't quite respond to aspirations but as Buc said, with philosophical good cheer, ''You can't win them all.''✤

An Important Announcement To Our Subscribers!

BACK ISSUES OF AUTOMOBILE QUARTERLY ARE GOING OUT OF STOCK AND WILL NOT BE REPRINTED!

This is the last offer being made exclusively to subscribers. Remaining issues will be offered next on the open market on a first-come, first-served basis, which can only elevate the price asked by collectors and individual sellers.

A complete set of *Automobile Quarterly* magazine is an unbeatable investment for monetary gain or informational value. Why pay more later? Issues are offered to subscribers with no attempt to take advantage of any issue's rarity.

Subscribers' Prices $9.95 Each

Your selection of
10 or more
any volumes, any years you
need to fill in your set

$9.00 Each

Including shipping, handling and insurance to points within USA on prepaid and credit card orders. (For overseas shipment, add $.50 per copy, $40.00 for complete set.)

Yes! Full sets are available.

Less than one hundred sets have been reserved for our subscribers. Sixteen volumes, sixty-four issues, four four-year indexes and seventeen slipcases — **SAVE $170.95. YOUR PRICE: $599.95** (Regular Price $760.95). A lot of money, true, but an excellent investment any way you look at it.

Indeed! We offer an Installment Plan.

Pay in three installments of $200.00 each. You may take up to nine months to pay—Just send us $200.00 and we will send you twenty-four issues (Volumes 1 through 6) with six slipcases; send your next payment of $200.00 and we will ship the next twenty-four issues (Volumes 7 through 12) with six slipcases. Upon receipt of your final payment of $200.00 we will ship the remaining twenty issues (Volumes 13 through 17 plus four four-year indexes and six slipcases).

Here are last month's inventory totals per volume:

The first to go out of print are Volume 1, Number 1 (1962) through Volume 10, Number 4 (1971), as previously announced. Regrettably, we can no longer maintain an inventory of all back issues, which, understandably, will now become rare and expensive, something we have tried to prevent in our objective of publishing the best available stories and history of the automobile. We urge subscribers to order today those missing copies while they last. Why pay more later? These back issues are available at our regular subscriber's discount price, with no attempt to take advantage of the issues' rarity.

Vol.	*Quan.	Vol.	*Quan.	Vol.	*Quan.	Vol.	*Quan.
1-1	3,250	3-3	3,178	6-1	2,380	8-3	380
1-2	309	3-4	1,429	6-2	2,967	8-4	420
1-3	1,463	4-1	1,666	6-3	1,160	9-1	460
1-4	1,973	4-2	2,500	6-4	740	9-2	1,502
2-1	1,798	4-3	400	7-1	1,170	9-3	430
2-2	1,528	4-4	430	7-2	560	9-4	979
2-3	2,500	5-1	1,300	7-3	2,500	10-1	1,070
2-4	1,600	5-2	880	7-4	455	10-2	3,446
3-1	530	5-3	690	8-1	2,500	10-3	1,090
3-2	2,440	5-4	1,528	8-2	3,180	10-4	3,345

*Quantity available as of October 1, 1979

Notes & Photo Credits

The author of our model car story, DAVID SINCLAIR, is a former advertising and sales promotion executive. In 1963 he pioneered the mail order sales of automotive miniatures in the United States. He owns an impressive collection of miniatures but, believing one's business and hobby should be separate, spends most of his spare time as an actor with several theatre groups in his hometown of Erie, Pennsylvania. Since January 1976 he has appeared on stage frequently, starring in such plays as *That Championship Season* and *Long Day's Journey into Night*.

The author of our Sammy Davis story, MICHAEL FROSTICK, was born the son of an English parson during the First World War and had his first motoring experience soon after. There is, or was, extant a photograph of him on an uncle's lap grasping the steering wheel of a 1914 Morris Oxford with one hand and his woolly hat with the other. Enthusiasm for motorcars followed through school. Accepted as an apprentice by the engineering firm of Harry Ricardo, he was sidetracked into the theatre where he quickly discovered he could not make a living and decamped to a London advertising agency which had the Austin account at the time. After a war of sticking his neck out of a Daimler armoured car from the Western Desert to Copenhagen, he returned to the theatre as press officer for the Royal Opera House, leaving to become associate editor of *Ambassador* magazine, where he immediately gave himself the additional appointments of aeronautical and motoring correspondent. Persuaded away from the magazine by Sol Hurok, he found himself for the next eight years representing a good slice of American musical and theatrical life in Europe. After a brief foray into television, he became the last administrator of the Old Vic before it officially became the National Theatre. Throughout this time he maintained his interest in motoring, writing for various journals and completing his first motoring book in 1955. With Louis Klemantaski he founded the motor racing magazine *Autocourse* and about that time began competing in national and international rallies. He did his first "Monte" in a Standard Vanguard in 1952 and has since done nine others. After formation of the National Theatre, he decided the best way to go on eating was a return to television and, realizing money is made in front of the camera and

not behind it, became a reporter on the BBC motoring program *Wheelbase*. When, after eleven years, the energy crisis brought this to an end, he became a consultant on collector cars to the auction house of Christie's, and continued writing motoring books, of which he has now published more than thirty. He divides his time between a tiny house in Surrey, where he is never off the telephone, and a farmhouse in Provence, where he is never off the typewriter.

FRONTISPIECE
Emblem from the 1909 E-M-F owned by Harold Worley and photographed by Roy Query.

E & M & F . . . & LEROY
340-341: From the left, E (Barney Everitt) and M (William Metzger) and F (Walter Flanders) and LeRoy, all portraits courtesy of the National Automotive History Collection of the Detroit Public Library. 342-343, 344-345, 348-349, 350, 352, 359: Photographs by Roy Query. 347, 351, 353, 354, 355, 356-357, 358: Photographs by Rick Lenz.

Special thanks from the author to her good friend George Risley who, over the course of her numerous visits to the Detroit Public Library, never failed to suggest the E-M-F idea. The story was a bushel of fun to do.

The Antique Studebaker Club, P.O. Box 142, Monrovia, California 91016.

OF FORDS AND FINNS
Our opening spread photograph shows Bo Ljungfeldt speeding over the Grand Prix course at Monte Carlo at the end of the 1964 Monte Carlo Rally. 364 above: Courtesy of Saab-Scania of America. 368 bottom: Courtesy of Jaguar Rover Triumph Inc. All other photographs courtesy of the author.

SAMMY
400: Photograph by Neill Bruce. 403: Courtesy of the National Motor Museum at Beaulieu. 406 below: Courtesy of *Autocar*. All other photographs from the personal albums of Sammy Davis.

With the car portraits they submit to us, our photographers submit as well a detailed Identification Sheet

with car and owner information for our captioning purposes. When he sent his portraits of Sammy for this article, Neill Bruce included the standardized identification form, suitably filled out. It's one of the many reasons working with Neill is such a pleasure, and we'd like to share it with you. "*Make:* Human. *Year:* 1887. *Model and/or type designation:* Racing cartoonist, S.C.H. Davis. *Body style:* Slight. *Coachbuilder:* Mrs. Davis (Victorian model). *Distinguishing characteristics (include color):* Small, white Caucasian; dark beret, whitish goat beard, 92 years old but doesn't look it, glasses. *Notes of interest:* Too numerous to list, but drove Bentleys, Austins, etc in the Golden years; won Le Mans; attributed to downfall of Invicta cars by crashing same at Brooklands in 1931. . . . *Owner:* Mrs. Davis (Elizabethan model)."

A LINCOLN FOR THE '80'S
Color photography by Stan Grayson. Design renderings and b/w photograph courtesy of Gail Halderman and the staff of Lincoln's public relations department.

MAURO FORGHIERI
Our opening spread shows Mauro Forghieri and Carlos Reutemann after practice for the German Grand Prix in 1978. 416, 419 above left, 420 below, 424 below, 425 right: Courtesy of D.P.P.I., Levallois. 418, 422 below left: Courtesy of Franco Zagari. 420 right: Photograph by Adriano Cimarosti. 425 below left: Courtesy of *Automobil Revue*. 424 above: Photograph by Pete Coltrin. All other b/w photos courtesy of the author. 426 top: Photograph by Pieter E. Kamp. 426 bottom: Photograph by Rick Lenz. 427, 428, 429: Photographs by Neill Bruce. 430, 431: Photographs by Stan Grayson.

The author would like to extend a special thanks to his British colleague, Jeremy Walton, for his assistance. The editors wish to thank Robert Dusek for his counsel.

THE ELUSIVE BUCCIALI
Our opening spread shows the crowded Bucciali stand at the 1930 Paris Show. The portrait of Lt. Paul-Albert Bucciali was done in 1918 when he was a member of Groupe des Cigognes. All b/w photographs courtesy of the author, Uwe Hucke, or from the AUTOMOBILE *Quarterly* collection.

The Bucciali emblem is debossed on our back cover.